FACES OF THE MOTHER

a journey · a collaboration · a feminine restoration

INKWATER PRESS

by SHARON ANN ROSE

with contributions from our Feminine Life Artists

"*Faces of the Mother* is a testament to the potency of the Divine Feminine that is resurging around the world. It intimately depicts the journey of a small group of artists through 13 feminine archetypes through deep sharing and beautiful imagery. Those who read this book can expect their own creativity to blossom as well."

~ DEVAA HALEY MITCHELL, SPIRITUAL GUIDE,
TRANSFORMATIONAL LEADER & INSPIRED MUSICIAN

"In these times of intense change – and resistance to change – in our world, women everywhere are being called by the Mother. That call comes from deep within their bellies, goes back as far as Life itself, and invites – or more often, demands – nothing less than a heart-full response. Sharon Ann Rose's *Faces of the Mother* is a beautiful example of one woman's response to that call, both in her personal journey and in the evolution of her work with women."

~ LYNDA TERRY, AUTHOR OF *THE 11 INTENTIONS: INVOKING THE
SACRED FEMININE AS A PATHWAY TO INNER PEACE*

"*Faces of the Mother* is a guide map to the process of allowance, surrender and transformation that is catalyzed by the Divine Feminine and her many forms. Sharon expresses eloquently the journey of her, and 11 other women's, sojourn into the mystery of creation and manifestation. Through the committed path of their journey, these women explored their doubt, unknowing and fear. Facing these aspects with courage and humility, they supported and midwifed each other into embodiment of their authenticity, creativity and power. This book is an inspiration as it conveys so well the power of the unification of women yearning for deeper connection with themselves and the Divine."

~ ROBIN BODHI-MCCULLOCH, HOLISTIC PRACTITIONER AND EMBODIMENT COACH

"All mothers need help and inspiration for one of the most important and challenging jobs in the world. In her new book, *Faces of the Mother*, Sharon shows women how to use their intuition and creativity to both care for their children and themselves in the highest way."

~ JOYCE VISSELL, CO-AUTHOR OF *THE SHARED HEART, MODELS
OF LOVE AND A MOTHER'S FINAL GIFT*

Publisher: Inkwater Press | www.inkwaterpress.com

Paperback ISBN-13 978-1-62901-355-8 | ISBN-10 1-62901-355-2
Kindle   ISBN-13 978-1-62901-356-5 | ISBN-10 1-62901-356-0

Printed in the U.S.A.

3 5 7 9 10 8 6 4 2

♡

To my mother, Jane Ann Kordana,
my love and devotion are with you always.

To Vicky York,
who pursued a life of abiding service to the nurturance of all Mothers.

And to the heart of the Mother within us all.

Contents

PART THREE
A FEMININE RESTORATION

Foreword

What does it mean to be a mother of the world?

I am sitting at the foot of the shrine of Mary, mother of Yeshua, at the Grotto in Portland, Oregon. My heart cracked open like a baby seedpod finding its way to the light.

In this place of solace, the Queen of Heaven has joined me in consuming chaos for breakfast, along with my usual cup of cosmic coffee. Etched in my heart's memory is the day when Sharon and I spent time here together, kneeling at her altar in both tears and ecstasy, in the awakening connection of our soul's calling. It is all that I can ask from my sister. It is she who has become my greatest ally, as we hold hands, pray and dive yet again into the holy mother wound. As a fellow soul searcher and devotee to the Path of She, it is here that I find myself in true surrender from the seemingly endless suffering of the world, the challenges of my personal life, and raising my own family as a motherless mother.

She must have the answer.

A few years ago, together on a walk in the woods behind Sharon's home, I dropped the 'big one' on her. Amidst the dense moss and trees of the primordial forest, I got up the nerve to ask her if she would 'initiate me' as a priestess.

Yup, I used the 'P' word.

Years later, she admitted to me that she was quietly terrified at the prospect at the time. We, as wild women, seem to have a knack for this, as we share a quest for ineffable truth. We each bow to, and respect one another as teachers, healers, artists and mothers. We spark within each other the flame of remembering who we really are. And the chord of shame that comes along with our light unveiled is a very real thing. As keepers of Her mysteries, we have seen Her name fallen along with us. Her temples destroyed by the patriarchal forces. The way of the holy mother as 'the Virgin' has become a somewhat untouchable thing. The tantric priestess a prostitute. We know these stories are etched into our genetic codes.

Lost unto herself, the reclamation of the Sacred Feminine has become our holy war cry. And so, I asked her as my mirror, because as a woman of the modern day world, where can I find Her again? Where do I find myself?

We are generational creatrixes, as we carry the eggs and seed potentials from our grandmothers and for our grandchildren. This is no small task. It doesn't matter if you have children or not. It is through the abiding by your own forsaken sense of self-pleasure in creation, and in listening to the waves of your sorrows as they arise and fall, which is your initiation. It is when we surf through our untamed urges and dive into our unexpressed inner longings that we discover Her, the Faces of the Mother.

The women that weave their stories throughout this book are our own inner voices, the lost treasures of our time. As caretakers of wonder, it is here that we are heard, held and witnessed, as we find that the gift within the things that plague us is where we also find our deepest passions. Even when we think the Light is more than we can bear, it is in those times where we can choose to save ourselves by cherishing our most vulnerable places.

What you have in your hands is a passage into the divine realms, a baptism into your essential *criatura*. It is a gateway to the Mother, who calls you home to your inner mastery. Sharon ever so gracefully anoints you into your beloved embodiment, as you join her in the eternal dance of love. She is the lioness butterfly, who will run and leap beside you as you decide to take this adventure into your soul's inner caverns. She is an earth wisdom keeper, a soul beacon for freedom, and a tamer of dragons... because you know she's been there and back again, and there is always more to discover!

Together we are re-wilding our hearts, learning to reweave our stories and sacred mythology, and thereby reclaiming the womb wisdom which is our collective evolution. By listening to our own spiritual purpose, we help others to discover their own. In so doing, we restore the ancient feminine mysteries that echo through our blood and bones, and along with that the living temple within.

I reflect back in contemplation to Mary, our mother, our sister, and our universal lover, Her most fragrant sacred rose heart revealed, open and bleeding.

She is Our Goddess, who loves beyond reason and without question. She is Lady Isis, Mother of Magick, the Cosmic Womb of Creation. She is both the Light and the Darkness who continues to unravel our psyche, and at the same time keeps us a disciple to our intimate truth. Her answer fills me with what feels like the rage of annihilation. Much like labor pains transmuted into pure creative force, she becomes the rapturous warmth and intense power of trusting what it means to truly live.

Here is a map to the lost gems of a woman's soul, which has come to you perfectly now and just in time. Know that if you are afraid at times, and you will be, it is a good sign. It means that true love is knocking on your door, and the wild tigress awaits.

Jasmin Soleil
INTUITIVE CONSULTANT, HEALER, WRITER & WILD MOON PRIESTESS
www.jasminsoleil.com

Beloved Daughter, You Were Never Lost

She believed she was lost.
She believed she was broken.
She believed she'd been burnt,
turned to ash
gone all soft and weak
because her way looked different.
Her way had been quiet
gone unseen
it hadn't left an indelible mark.

Her way had brought forth things
easily blown away by the wind,
and tenderly washed into a vast merging sea.

She hadn't cared about riches
of a modern world -
about growth, money, having-the-last-say.
She'd cared about her children and sisters,
about family and love
about her husband and his heart's healing
and the earth she longed so deeply
to tread gently upon.

She believed she was now worn out
and weathered down
no longer having anything of purpose or value left
to share with the world
because she HAD cared about things that go unspoken, unseen
about humanity
and this place we call home.
And this invisible beauty,
it doesn't match up
with what the world has claimed
GORGEOUS.

So she went to where she was most drawn
and rested awhile in the searing sun,
leaning into the trees, soil and earth,
listening to wind and stream.

And here, she heard a rhythm.
A subtle song she knew others could hear
if they were listening.
If they were listening!

Would she trust this voice and wisdom again?

Life's beauty, it's indefinable.
Life's worth, it's uncontainable.
The world has no way to recognize it.
It can't be seen through the methods we've been taught to see what's most precious.

But you, my love.
You can hear it. You have seen it. You have held it... so deeply to your breast,
this truth of all nations
of all hearts.
This richness that lives in the core of our blood and breath, giving life to each moment
if we let it.

If we let it.

And so...
the hands of love carried Her back,
from the embrace of the Mother and Father's undying unity.

And She knew she would rest here.
She'd offer what she came to.
To stand beside her Sisters
at home, together.
Love's holiest daughters.

A Love Letter

Asustaining relationship often begins with a sincere love letter... an expression of one's deepest honesty and a testament to our own vulnerability. And so it is here I begin, offering these proclamations of my heart to you...

Dearest Reader,

Can you hear Her calling? Can you hear Her calling *you* home?

Home. Into the home of our bodies and lives. Into the home where we know and recognize ourselves and each other as She does... as whole, pure, precious to life and unified with it all.

We've been woven into a communal tapestry, deep through the soil of our personal and collective restoration. And as a result of this inter-dynamic existence, this book and its soulful expression came to life as plots of our hearts were hoed and rich humus turned over, offering an exposed concentration of nutrition from this mutual honoring, healing, believing in and engaging with our personal creative rhythms and collective insights. I yearned and chose to listen to *this* pulsation of nature's universal course.

I've been calling out to Her. I've been calling out to Love.

We've been reaching out for Her. We've been reaching out to Life.

I wrote this journeybook because I believe in you. And in writing it, I learned to believe in myself. And herein I watched how 'We' is born.

This story and its birthing process comes from a place so far down within me and the matter of life, I couldn't think my way through. To access this material I encountered a darkness so rich, deep, enigmatic and dense. There were no flashlights to turn on, and when I tried, She told me not to reach for a light. I had no translation for it and knew I'd simply need to plunge in and discover what was resting here. I faced layers of residue, mold and cobwebs, and the ensuing tenderness it takes to resurrect ancient places that have been locked up and proclaimed of no value or benefit.

To discover the root intention for writing this book, I had to fully bring it to life, calling its breath forth from the marrow of my blood, bones and history... feeling its aliveness and landscape in the cells and nature of my soul's creativity and expression. I had to believe what I felt arising mattered, and that somehow, someday, you would come and this process would be of benefit.

We've been living together in these deeper places and their resultant knowing. We've journeyed through its darkness distinctly and in partnership, and have been made and then remade from the seamless fabric of our mutual heart. I had to trust the persistent visions I saw and ensuing sensations I felt. In the caverns of our darkness before life existed, we were walking side-by-side through all we've forever been aching for. I chose to believe what was arising within me was real. I trusted my life would grow from it.

Early on in this process, a woman who read the original manuscript asked, "Why did you write it? What do you hope to achieve?" I sense she was picking up on my own insecurity of purpose, as still I stumble for what this book is, and continue to come up against the deeper sense and authenticity that *this* cannot be defined through my or any of the world's outer constructs.

The basic premise for this book is that I believe in life and love, and in our creative capacity to transform through the forgiveness that arises as we gently cradle our humanity, past choices and ensuing suffering. I wrote this book to forgive myself... to forgive all parts of me that believed I wasn't enough, didn't have anything to say, or would never have anything to offer or be able to fit in. I wrote this book to grieve for these lost years of not believing in my soul and its worth, and to grieve for the collective years of our lost humanity. Of not trusting and following our deepest heart's longing. Of being afraid to give *everything* we have to resurrect our innocence and creativity.

In the Mother's arms, all this is held with knowing and compassion. And this is where I place the purpose of this book.

Through this journey of incomprehensible self-acceptance, I discovered I was writing simply because I was! And I could. I discovered I was writing because I can share what I can share. I can write what I can write, and express what I can express. The grand humor and deepest honesty of this discovery is I *don't* have anything new to say, because *we all feel* what I have come to know. And I *won't ever* fit in, because my creativity is unique, as is yours, and our sacred expression *is the cauldron* through which life flows. It can't be constrained by anything that has come before. I will never *be enough*, because I do not exist alone or in separation, or without you, and we are growing this life together.

Through accepting these sacred and simple human conditions, I welcomed an immense freedom to create because I can create in the way I create... and for no other reason. Our creativity and expression will *never* FIT IN. It is the foundation from which all of life flows. It is what everything FITS INTO and POURS OUT OF. We are meant to create as only we can and do because we are truly boundless and free to be ourselves.

The truth is, I didn't write *Faces of the Mother* to change you or the world. I wrote it to accept the changeless in myself. There are things we are not meant to overcome. There are places in us we are not meant to transform. There are aspects of our world we are not meant to heal or perceive as needing to be healed.

Dearest Reader, this is where my love letter to you begins.

May this book offer a sincere glimpse into a condition that no longer judges life, ourselves and how we create from such limited notions of control, manipulation and determination of the pathways of our existence and creativity.

From the deepest place in my being, I share this work because I wish to share what lives within. In so doing, may it bless you in being you.

Anything you read here or that I may say in the future about this book's creation will always come back to this... I wrote this because I wanted to connect deeply with the world from the depth that I am. And in that process I learned how to create an everlasting forgiveness for it all. I wonder if you will too?

And like a child, I wanted to see what might *then* unfold...

With my undying love,

Sharon Ann Rose xo

An Insider's Perspective

Dear Reader,

I had the honor of reading Sharon's manuscript for *Faces of the Mother* twice. Initially I just read it through, and then was asked to proofread it. In that process I realized two things: first, I was inspired by Sharon's courage in facing the personal growth required for her own transformation before she could bring this material to other women; secondly, how much deeper it penetrated into my body and soul, heart and womb, the second time around. When I finished the second reading, I felt the desire to pick it up a third time and go directly to the Faces that spoke most to me, review them, and decide which Face I wanted to work with.

It doesn't seem to matter how young or old one is; there's something for each of us in this book and process. If you're a young woman feeling called to explore your relationship with the Feminine, if you're a middle-aged woman looking for a deeper understanding of yourself, or if you are an elder woman reviewing ways to see what you may have missed as you grew up in the old patriarchal paradigm, you can find gems to honor you and continue your transformational process here. There is a lot of value in this book for those who are serious about going deeper, and it's an inspiring story about Sharon's courage in taking on this project.

I found Sharon's description of the heart-womb dynamic in each of us intriguing. This feels like a really important point, and one I had never thought of. Regardless of age, we are all being called to create ourselves anew. Whether gestating a baby or a more evolved version of ourselves, *it is crucial to create.* As the world shifts, more women like you will be drawn to this work, and all who are drawn to it have the potential to change at a deep level as Sharon did. I really honor her courage and commitment to the personal work, the work with others, and putting this experience into book form.

You may want to consider—and I highly recommend—reading this book more than once. As happened for me, reading it once for the overview of the process, a second time to get deeper into the concepts, and a third time to really work with one or more *Faces of the Mother* gives you the opportunity to see how She can transform you. A word of caution: if you find the first introductory section slow reading, stick with it, please! It is so important to understand the whole process. I guarantee you will find it worth your while.

As women, we often spend more time committing ourselves to others' needs than to our own. It is time to support our own growth and stay committed, trusting the Feminine to work through us. It's a multi-layered process going deeper and deeper that takes time and courage, but the commitment is worth it as the transformation occurs. Are you willing to begin?

Karen Latvala
LIFE COACH AND VESSEL OF THE DIVINE FEMININE

An Introduction

Mother of the Woods

I make my way into the forest across from our home. It's early summer, in the morning; my 1-½ year old dog is at my side. Over the past 12 years I've sojourned into these woods for solitude and restoration. I've come to this sanctuary in the wilds for ceremony and collaboration, with my friends, circles of women, children and families, and with the deepest truths of my own heart. Here I've walked with our family dogs that have since passed on, and been on walks with forgotten parts of me I now remember. I've trekked with my 3 boys, stumbling over felled logs and bramble, forging new pathways through the trees. I've watched my sons follow the call of the wild, building tree forts, playing capture the flag and hide-n-seek with friends. Those in my family have known this forest as an extension of our yard. I have known it as an extension of my own breath and body.

Today I head towards a tree that's been a beacon of guidance. A trusted friend in my hardest hour. A wise counsel when I couldn't see my way. My children and I once named Her, "Mother of the Woods." This endearment has remained. I pull a small token out of my pocket. It is time to honor a cycle passing.

I place the clear glass medallion with a tree image decoupaged on it, in the belly of the tree's base. I say a prayer and offer a blessing. I am letting go... of a feeling, a life lesson, an immense heartache and golden gift. No longer can I discern where it comes from or whose face it belongs to. In the presence of the one I know as the Mother of the Woods, my story is heard and no longer matters. I bend down placing my hand on the moss covering Her trunk. I breathe and let go. I trust She will take what no longer serves me.

Feminine Manifestation

It is mid-July of 2013. I have welcomed a circle of women to join me on a 3-month internal pilgrimage into the creative terrain of our being to discover what has barred and supported our feminine wisdom and its expression. A gentle rhythm and grounded structure has come forth. We will connect via pathways of the heart and soul, and through email, phone and audio exchanges. Joined in the landscape of our feminine spirit, our shared purpose is to create expressive faces of the Mother as we have and will come to know Her.

I am not sure what lies ahead. I breathe and let go. I trust She will guide us where we will most be served.

I'm now 42 years old, on my way into the infamous mid-life. Many have claimed it's a time of crisis. I've discovered it's a season for rebirth. Through this milestone I've reflected on my purpose, harnessing my creative fire and delving in to the shadowy trenches of my past. For over 15 years I've worked with women and mothers, learning about, healing and discovering a deeper truth we carry into the nature of creation. A profound wisdom rests inside our feminine being. I know it scares us. It has petrified me. And it is what prompts us forth. I want to uphold what it takes to completely trust, revere and wildly abandon to this.

I pause for a breath. I am ready to carve a new path, to follow the deepest truth through this terrain. I will go where it leads, even if I am afraid.

My work has been devoted to exploring the field of Feminine wisdom. I've served and excavated the depths of Her soul, coming up against unworldly heart-ache, seeing sides to pleasure, joy and sincerity that our culture has no idea what to do with. With this circle of women by my side, we will travel to realms there are no words for, treasuring what we find and accepting it as a gift. We will bring it back to bless our hearts and all of life.

I am not sure what lies ahead. I breathe and let go. I trust She will guide us where we will most be served.

To the ancient and innocent relationship with the Mother I offer this journey. She is both an iconic and religious figure I have felt intimate with since child-hood, and is the energy I find in the Earth below and around me, in the eyes of my husband and children, in the warmth of a friend's embrace, and in the folds of a flower strewn hilltop, an expanse of ocean, in the breath of a flea. She is the welcoming I discover as I come home to myself.

The relationship we hold with the Great Mother lives within and around us. It brings us to life and ushers the force of creation through our bodies and relations. We know this in the caverns of our being. We come into existence trusting and allowing its energy to guide our way. And along our path we naturally forget, innocently enraptured by the beauty, glitz and glimmer that surrounds us, taking our attention off the beauty, purpose and truth that lives within.

How quickly we move from *being* the raw force of life to *believing* we have to manipulate, control and individually create or purpose it. How quickly we draw our attention outward to follow an externally-focused culture purporting creation is something that occurs outside of and separate from us, and that manifestation happens through something we can individually spearhead.

I'd like to share another side to this story. *Faces of the Mother* was created to support and honor what we carry deeply within. This book is an offering, validity and healing for the truth orchestrated through our inherent Feminine way. This is where we come together in the land of pure creation. Here we remember we are breathing as one for all, and all for one.

Beginning... before it began

My life is a testament to the wonders of the whole. All that I do carries blessings for you within it. And I am clear that all you do, honors and blesses me intrinsically. This is the landscape of our mutual thriving. This validates the truth about how life works... in eternal togetherness.

Faces of the Mother began long before an invitation was sent out calling Feminine Life Artists forth to travel autonomously and in collaboration into the uncharted creative feminine of our being. This collection came together before any person put pen to paper, brush to canvas, notes to song or words into form. This journey was initiated before a vision appeared, an intention harnessed or purpose ignited. *Faces of the Mother* set into motion long before I knew what was going to occur.

This collection has been shaping through all time. I see this book and its creative formation as the result of years of aching and lifetimes of longing for a deeper, tangible way to relate to and express the union we hold within, and to cherish the truths of the mystery of our creation. Through unbeknownst passages quite simply back to the beginning before it all began, *Faces of the Mother* was initiated.

It has been shaping through soul longings rising and intrepid commitment rooting to face whatever it would take to form from within our expression of inner union, power, creativity, wisdom and grace... each person's own Face *as* the Mother. And then here, through these women you will come to soulfully know, something was heard, coalesced and made known. A primordial sound far beyond the reaches of what we can define, rose inside the hearts and wombs of us all, and *Faces of the Mother* formed.

Women came forth. Feminine Life Artists revealed. Paintings were created. Paintings were painted over. Words written, photographs taken, inner resistances greeted. Drawings sketched, souls coalesced and distinct paths forged. Dances were sweated, fires burned, and cocoons constructed. Clarity was lost, self was found, wild prayers offered, surrender awakened. Studios cleared, songs forgotten, rhythms remembered, tears fallen and masks peeled away...

Here is the story of how She came alive. And here you are, the perfect integral piece.

This book is a celebration of how She is coming alive through us all...

WELCOME TO

FACES OF THE MOTHER

a journey · a collaboration · a feminine restoration

Orientation

I want to orient you a bit to this process, so you can feel the fluidity required to delve in to the passage ahead.

Often in our culture, we're asked to get straight to the point. To lay it on the line and state in as few words as possible what something is going to be about. We want to get where we think we're *supposed* to be going as quickly and efficiently as possible. And yes, this does serve an important function, and it pleases our mind immensely to have immediate satisfaction and answers.

And yet, the passage of our hearts and souls is not satisfied with such immediacy and directness. The deeper wisdom of our being is meandrous and poetic, offering us riches that cannot be grabbed in a moment's notice, but rather, discovered and savored bit by bit as we settle in and let go, and don't try so hard to get where we think we *should* be going. This is the path of noticing where we *actually* are.

I've lived through too much and seen the effects of this fast-paced directness and what it can do to one's soul... especially to the heart of the Feminine. So I know... you might get pretty antsy here. In the beginning, you might start saying to yourself, "Would you just *get on* with this already?!" I'm willing to take the heat for this one. Too much is at stake. Your heart and soul, my love, can only be ignored for so long.

So dear reader please let go. And breathe. And join me here on this meandering pathway of moving deeply in to your senses and feelings, and in to what the heart of She has in store.

View from a Tree

This book you're now holding... it's got breath and aliveness. So go ahead! Take a moment and breathe with and into it as it rests in your own hands.

Faces of the Mother is a journey of our mutual creation. It's not a static or sedentary expression. It's like a newborn bird I've been tenderly holding in my hands. I'm sitting in a resilient nest high atop a magnificent tree looking out upon the vast landscape that is all of creation. I am rooted in the unseeable domain that extends far below ground, connecting all of life and each of us together in this moment.

I look at this bird. I know it is meant to fly. I feel it in my bones, in searching fingers that grasp softened wing feathers, in the quaking of my heart thrumming inside my chest.

I look at this bird. I am struck by its crystal clear black eyes, a softened gaze that is open, innocent and ready for what cannot be known.

There is part of me that is not ready to let this bird go. To hand it to you and see *where* it will go, allowing its deepening journey into the vastness of creation. I breathe fully. I may never be ready in the way I imagine one should. I am ready in the way that only I am.

I am now this tender newborn bird readying for flight. And I am the holder of this bird, choosing when to set it free. How and in what ways will I honor the wind and sun, the weather, and the seasons in which it will fly forth? I contemplate. I remember. I breathe. I allow the fullness of this process, gifting it here into the beginning of our passage. Gifting it here into *your* hands so you can sense the deeper places where this all began and is going, and then choose to do what you will do with it.

To share the sincere creations of our heart and soul is an utterly terrifying, vulnerable and most essential component to fully living. It is here we discover we already know how to fly. Soaring from the vast limbs of a tree, we catch a downwind and backwards glance at the tree's breadth, seeing what we've been held and carried by all along. Somehow, in some way, through this flight we find peace. It settles into our bones like an old remembrance as we exhale into ourselves... into who we and are created to be.

And here, we learn to let go...to gift our gifts to others without turning back.

Faces of the Mother begins in the throes of this indescribable flight. Filled with trepidation and wonder, with complexity and entanglement, with a deep hope for humanity's most noble self-expression and how this is and *will* set all of life free. And it begins in my trust... of myself, of you... and of this life we are growing together.

Our life's passage brings us high amongst treetops and deep into the bellows of the roots again and again. These journeys take us to vast horizons and back to where it all begins for a rich and significant purpose. Like inhalation and exhalation. Like an adventure's circuitous wandering without a preset destination. The passage itself gives a broader and sometimes terrifying perspective of our choice in each moment and the consequence of our actions. This is the landscape of our most primordial existence. This is where the creativity of our lives takes shape, is born and set free.

There is an ancient and evolutionary wisdom in this passage. *Faces of the Mother* draws upon this as our orientation. Resting atop a magnificent tree at a moment right before flight, ahhhh... breathing, we choose to let the bird go.

Listening... roots of this journey

As we stop resisting the deeper nature of life and repetitive wisdom of our wounds and healing, we discover a vast and rich terrain. Here we find a presence within that doesn't run from ourselves, choosing to make space again and again as we dive deeper to watch, witness, listen and contemplate from where we come and are going. It is *through* this journey we allow ourselves to become its living mystery. And we begin to grow as the rooted faith we've been externally searching for. This is what allows us to share what we came to this world to share.

It is here we orient to who we uniquely and collectively are. And we listen... listen to our bodies, hearts, our wombs and bellies, our souls, the earth, our source and one another.

We can choose to listen. To listen to life and the artistry of our inherent living, resting in this tree that has incorruptible faith in our interconnection with it all.

Let us look and listen together.

This book and its preceding journey arose from listening to my own persistent and deepest longing. These longings, the deepest ones, they carry our true purpose. And mine is to intimately feel, know, bring forth, share, believe in and serve what I've sensed the archetypal and living Mother contained and offered. Yet everywhere I turned (in my outer world and inner perceptions) I came up against a single-sided, limited, one-size-fits-all replication.

Through my childhood I saw the Mother through the lens of religious expression – our Divine Mother – all caring, virginal, silent, a holy vessel. As I grew, I saw Her through the mothering of modern society, ignored, devalued and avoided, displayed through the worn-down feminine raising children and life in a culture that discredited and banished what couldn't be proven, make a profit, or turned into a product.

As a young girl looking for the living confirmation of a startling power she knew she personally held within, the women I saw around me offered little guidance or direction for how to access the deeper truth I felt and had no idea how to contain. I witnessed a generation working to uphold the ideal of a chaste, all compassionate, never fully fulfilled Feminine. Or the can-do-it-all, self-sustaining, face it head-on woman that didn't equate with my inner reality. This brought me to my knees, into my exhaustion and a deeper journey of contemplation, inner connection and personal intimacy.

Faces of the Mother comes from and engages these deepening questions into the relationship we hold with creation itself, "How do I express what cannot be expressed?" "How do I share the full scope of that which *is* the full scope and I am but *one* part?" "How do you depict the true face and wisdom of the Mother as She comes alive through every aspect of creation?" And "How do I find the courage to share how She is awakening through me each step of the way?"

I can't. So why write this book?!

Listen. There is the desire; there will always be the desire. If we are honest, we realize we must follow it until we get to where the next moment reveals and some aspect of our longing is met. The true longing, our ultimate longing... may not be fulfilled in the way we imagine. It is why we live on. It is what prompts us to show up and keep giving all that we are. It is the reason you've been drawn to this journey and why I've taken the time to depict it. It is how and why we continue to come together... to breathe, in connection, collaboration, in community, into our bellies, with our source and as one family. It is what brings us alive, fueling our passion from deep within, helping us source our own breath from an inner purpose and conviction.

In following this felt sense I was drawn to call upon the creative expression of others to affirm and reveal what I knew is as common to us as life itself – our intimacy with our source and creation. I knew this would help me remain accountable to myself and to this unquenchable longing. Through my work in the realms of the soul, I knew we are the living reflection of life. By honoring what lives within, we personally taste love's uncontainable freedom. This is the ultimate task of sharing ourselves, offering our creative expression into the world so we might liberate the personal expression of all.

Within us the wisdom of the Mother comes alive through all aspects of our nature. And *Faces of the Mother* is a celebration that we are listening! And listening deeply. No longer are we choosing to clamp down, pigeonholing our existence, maiming our creativity, or butchering the love wanting to awaken through our world and us. We can choose to fly, to wait and wonder, to listen and let go. We can express our becoming no matter its form, face, rhythm or function. It *all* has magnificence and significance.

Engaging with the living Mother inside of us is how we access the bottomless pit of humanity's eternal creativity. It is inexhaustible because it is born of us, woven into the fabric of our breath, relationships, lives, organs, wisdom and skin. She is found beyond and within the lines and dimensions, beyond and within our preconceived notions and forms, imbued into every aspect of what we've known and can draw upon for soulful livelihood.

This is a heart aching journey of living and feeling who we are and long to be every step of the way. In working with the rhythms of creation we listen to the impulse of our inherent fertility (our creativity), choosing to pursue this sacred legacy. We can offer it to the world through all that will come and has been, through all that we are and can be.

And this is how I offer it to you. Through the gift and mission of this book.

And the truth is, this journey is not solitary, nor is the crafting and existence of this book. It requires our resilient togetherness, authentically expressing and learning, living and breathing through the love we are born of until the end of time.

What a monumental commitment – to discover our inner living faith. The journey of *Faces of the Mother* showed me that. And now, here at the threshold of making this first step for you... will you commit? Really!? And keep going? The first step... it's going to be simple. And we'll be ready for the next, since we've already begun our way. Will you trust yourself?

Let us begin here together now, witnessing an ancient wheel of our humanity turn. We've been here before. We will arrive yet again. There is no need to try so hard to get off and run from this spinning. There is no need to go anywhere. This tree of life reaches to touch everything. May we enter this landscape that is incomprehensible, yet fully accessible, to discover we bless and are blessed by life and everything within it.

From this view at the top of the tree you are free to soar with and for all of creation. What's important to *you* to explore? Where would you like to go?

Trusting the Tree

Our longings can take us to scary places... into those aspects of ourselves we don't really want to look at or admit we carry. And yet it's because of these desires we are carried to the threshold of our greatest genius... into those places that until we're willing to tenderly hold in our hands and gaze at face to face, we can not serve the world in the courageous and most natural way we are each meant to.

This has been the relationship I've had with writing and with this book. To be a writer is my greatest longing, deepest fear, and the true source of my genius. Working with this aspect of expression has been petrifying and more natural than anything I've ever known.

To write the book you now hold has been excruciating and liberating. Each time I sat down to write, it was a deep homecoming and a battle with judgments claiming how incapable I was. To continue forth, I learned to trust and make peace with this intricacy of opinions (mine, my ancestors' and upbringing's), praying to find a path through the forest so what I share may shed light and aid the ceasefire on our deepest suffering, on any residual distrust of the natural processes of growth, evolution, ourselves and our inherent expression.

This is no small task, though incredibly simple once you commit. I thank you for joining me in its potent, living dynamic where all things naturally unify – into our deepest vulnerability, into our most authentic truth, and into our pure simplicity of being. Through this writing a tender, real place within me now welcomes it all. Come, walk by my side. You, in your fullness, are welcomed here too.

I guarantee this will be a safe passage, though at times more dank and dark than you've ever known. May you remember you stand before this tree, calling upon its vast resilience. You are the tree. Breathe often and circulate its vitality. Absorb the sun into your belly whenever you're drawn to. Dig deep into your roots, as far as you're willing. This sustenance will carry you. It's available and sustainable because it's generated from inside and lives within you for always. Can you trust it?

Watching the Wind Blow... engaging our longing

Maybe this will come as no surprise, yet I offer this information now to open a doorway ever wider to what this journey can become for you. I did not enter the *Faces of the Mother* project with a thought-out agenda. I proceeded forth knowing I wanted, and deeply felt prompted, to share about the collective and intimate creative process and what has barred and will open its way. I chose the format of trusting the face of the feminine and its expression through me and the Life Artists you'll get acquainted with, as a way to live into the complexities, universalities and truths of what's been going on within the landscape of our inherent fertility... within the capacity we each have to co-create life and offer it to all.

Through a 3-month intensive journey that began in July 2013 and ended in October the same year, I stood beside a collective of women as they grappled with resistance, self-doubt and their inner saboteur. I wept for and with them as they felt past hurts, hurtling into bottomless darkness. I quietly and overtly proclaimed their victories as each woman found her own breath could carry her into fresh and unchartered territory and a deeper sense of who she truly is. Together these women and I sat in circle, peering upon works of genius created through their own hearts and hands, voices, womb visions and life's unfolding. I looked in awe as each woman walked her unique path, reflecting an ancient story and new discovery of herself and the Sacred Feminine within us all.

I've come to directly experience and witness the thwarting of our creative genius and its expression is what creates the dire world conditions we now face. The link between sharing our inner gifts and wisdom, and the starvation, deprivation, insanity and devaluation we now know as every-day reality, is intimately interconnected. And all this intertwines with how we engage with our feminine nature... with how we gestate and birth life, nurture and sustain our creativity and vision, and relate to one another, sharing our life's purpose for the well-being of all.

I recently read that as a child, Adolf Hitler wanted to be an artist, but he was not supported to explore or pursue this. Imagine how different our collective history would be if this man had been supported to believe in and share his inner gifts right from the beginning? Imagine how different our personal history would be if we valued our own feminine nature and organic creativity?

We can reflect on this historical time and person, inviting the deeper truths of this scenario to imbue us with new possibility and healing, and to ask ourselves, "What of our own childhood dreams have gone ignored and unsupported for far too long?" Adolf Hitler was an artist, yet he was not validated or supported in it, and thus didn't value it in himself. What we do not value about ourselves grows hard and cold, terrorizing us from the inside, eventually expressing itself out into the world in painful and traumatic ways. As a life artist, Hitler was driven to create. And so he poured all that creative possibility into designing one of the most horrific experiences of our personal and collective humanity, harnessing the notion of separation, individualization and hierarchy to place human against human in a battle for external authority and self-directed manifestation. The impact of his creativity and the power of his artistic longings were channeled through ways and means that will live inside our psyches and history books forever. Until we each personally commit to changing this.

May we honor that we are artists of our lives; here to share the expression of what we know to be blessed and beautiful from within ourselves. All we create is interwoven into the fabric of our life and humanity. Our lives matter more than we will ever know.

We are born to create. We will continue to create, irrespective of *what* we create. It is a natural impulse which some are more expressive of than others. Irrespective of the magnanimity of our expression, our creations impact us all on every level of existence. How, why and where we are creating from is far more important than what we produce in the end. We are all gifted, prolific creators of life. How will you channel and allow this forth?

Let us pause here, breathe and consider the impact this can and will have on every aspect of our lives, systems and structures. On our education, learning, health, relationships, spiritual connection and family. May we deeply allow what longs to unfold from the realms of our inherent way and vitality to do so. May we trust life's longings for us to be real.

Really! How different might your life be if you were supported to believe in and share your style of beauty and sacred expression... to value it with everything you've got? What would it be like if we simply 'put it out there' because we can!? To reveal to the world what the face of love looks like to and through us. Imagine!

Let's pass this gift along and make it real here and now. It can be hard to accept that the whole world depends on each of us sharing who we truly are. Trust me, it does.

Thus the mission of this book cannot be understated.

There are 4 key areas at the root and overflowing passion of this book's writing:

- To support and validate the natural creative process (what I term Soul Fertility). Helping us attune to and value this across all areas of existence. In the hearts, wombs and minds of mothers, women, men, in partnerships, families, communities and in our children.

- To empower us to heed the call of the Life Artist within as new structures upon the earth and throughout our social systems are born.

- To collectively access the wisdom of our Creative Feminine (our inherent initial natural order), allowing this to be our core infrastructure, so we are supported in learning and knowing that the way we connect with the inner wisdom of our being, with our creative genius and source intimacy, is *everything* to life! It is what restores deeper purpose, meaning, connection and love to our lives.

- To celebrate this as an interconnected process. This is where the mutuality of our existence comes alive. We create and manifest out of a shared field of wisdom that is gifting and imbuing us with the vitality of creation as we attune to and express it through our inherent gifts. This is a palpable field we can and are tapping in to as we work with our inherent fertility to bring forth new creation.

The mission of this book is large in its scope and impact, yet simple in its presentation and process. Amongst these pages you'll find a voyage that is deeply personal, yet fully encompassing. It is a modern portrayal and ancient reclamation of the vast yet simple mysteries of creation.

Faces of the Mother draws from and freshly reveals the collective creative experience life truly is. Without each other we might never know ourselves or fully experience the vastness of the divine. The ensuing words, stories, expressions, experiences, offerings, wisdom and prayers draw upon and forth a rich feminine legacy that celebrates all that has gone before and is yet to come. This is the way of the Feminine. Here we embrace and remain in connection to every detail and minutia of life. Here we honor we live for one another and belong to it all.

Weaving Together

At this point if it feels like you're head is spinning, and you aren't really clear what this book is going to be about, that's fine. Just breathe. And breathe some more. This is a journey. And it's *your* journey. This is preparation before the passage. If we're honest about what we *do* know, we just can't know what lies ahead. This is the landscape of our feminine fertility and life artistry. Breathe and surrender into this. Please.

And hunker in. This book is a voyage and shared collaboration. A circle of women has gone before you to discern this path and way, yet we now turn back to see the landscape and discoveries *you* will create by its passing to bless us all.

This book is personal and it is collective. It is part heroine's journey, and part adventure story of a group of intrepid explorers who paved a way for others to find themselves in their own way. This is a weaving of inner wisdom and a prompting to come into one's own truth. It's an invitation to celebrate, and the revelation of a celebration already underway. It is an opening into one's personal magic – art in its wildest sharing *and* most restrained limitations. It is a depiction and how-to-create your own feminine reclamation, and the sacred honor that comes from supporting others in the landscape of their creative soul fertility.

This book is the biography of a Feminine Life Artist through many expressions, and an invitation to know yourself *in* its vast reflection. Thank you for embarking upon this pilgrimage into the soil of the Feminine and what awaits when you're willing to dig deep, dive deeper, and keep going until you've touched the fullness of yourself through it all.

Faces of the Mother is a poetry of our heart, a portrait of our womb, and the depiction of the many facets of our nature as we surrender to the love that knows no bounds. This is the living, breathing depiction of what trust and inherent faith in ourselves and each other can do.

This book begins with the story of a creative fertility crisis for one woman, and moves into the journey of a circle of ancient, yet new friends and how they navigated their soul fertility. *Part One: A Journey* lays the landscape of how, why and where *Faces of the Mother* came into being, and outlines the structure of our process, giving you insight into the context of our passage. It shares an insider's perspective on what it takes to follow your creative genius, and portrays the initiations you will encounter as you commit to your fullest feminine expression.

Part Two: A Collaboration moves into the expression and sharing of our Mother Faces, the 13 living archetypes of the Mother that we worked with to discover the richness of our inherent Feminine Artistry. In this section you'll meet 10 fellow explorers who dug deep to embrace their soul fertility. Their creative expressions are shared, as well as snapshots into their personal journey. Through this section you'll be invited into your living relationship with the many Faces of the Mother as we provide ideas, artistry and questions to deepen this process within.

The final section of this book, *Part Three: A Feminine Restoration*, shares what occurred after our *Faces of the Mother* journey ended and how the behind-the-scenes compilation of this book took shape. It was during this time I got to live fully into what it takes to make this passage your own, following it homeward inside one's being, into the depths of our hearts. Here you'll receive unshakable support and commitment for bringing forth what you came to this life to birth into being.

May you no longer doubt your soul's deepest wisdom and creative fertility.

Final Tenderizing

Let me be upfront: this book is my attempt at offering you the wonders of creation, to share with you the living Faces of the Mother. This book is a glimpse at that which cannot be captured from the outside, only embraced on the inside. If I'm going to honor my commitment to transparency, you are its living face. A book of mirrors would aptly apply here. *Faces of the Mother* is a backdrop and YOU are the cover.

The visual and written expressions within this book are a peek at and gentle pulling back of a veil to discover a more comprehensive truth at what it means to be embraced and touched by love. This is a heart opening passage and invitation to dig through any self-judgment that says, "I am too small and unworthy to be cared for so deeply." Or to be honest about the aspects in us that proclaim, "I am too large and important to admit the value of our interconnected way." As we vulnerably open to what is within and before us, everyone comes to know and create love through it all.

And this requires our togetherness.

On behalf of *Faces of the Mother*, this collection is offered from humble hearts and courageous proclamations that *know* what we're attempting simply cannot be done, and yet it must. We must try with everything we have to share the small, mundane, unquenchable, gigantic and enormous, take-your-breath-away, intimate moments we've each experienced that bring us to our knees and help us rise again. We must share, live and breathe the many Faces of the Mother as our own. In this we are born. In this we live like children, playing together with and for the beauty of life.

Here we see the simple truth that we are family. Every one of us matters to us all.

PART ONE
A JOURNEY

Feminine Life Artistry... our sacred alchemy

Faces of the Mother began from the wisdom that it is sacred artistry to create our lives from our feminine essence. This is our birthright as women and humans, to reach for, touch, share, reveal and express the inherent and organic wisdom of creation from deep within. The workings of manifestation, nature and life live inside our bodies, blood and organs, and propel us into direct relationship with the truth of where we come from, who we are, how we came to be, and what will carry us into sustained and vital livelihood.

Through the *Faces of the Mother* process, I wanted to gain deeper perspective on what provides and fully supports, and what can and has blocked, the natural flow of the feminine through the expressions and creations of women and mothers. I wanted to be in service to each woman's unique path through the life artistry of herself... to support her reaching inside and fully expressing what she came to this earth to share. I wanted to help others and support myself to touch this treasured place that nothing else ever has.

A Feminine Life Artist is one who knows she is a representation of the mysteries of creation and the living force of the Mother. Through her life artistry, unique style and way of sharing, she offers her gifts and wisdom from the direct relationship she holds with the living vitality of love. Through her, she creates its face over and over through 10,000 ways and forms. To be a Feminine Life Artist is to follow the impulse of creation from deep inside.

This is no small undertaking. It requires a steadfast commitment to know oneself against all odds. It requires a complete reworking of our inherent relationship with not only the Feminine, but with the Masculine nature of our being. This results in our expression of unification. Here we allow the fatherly, focused, self-commitment of our unique, personal nature to be the protector for the flowering of our universal, motherly, expressive sacred self to unfold.

Through our *Faces of the Mother* journey we were consciously and unknowingly working with eons of past and current judgment around expressing ourselves as women, artists, co-creators and Mothers. And these are the most undervalued components of our society! Next to the state we hold for our children, elders and the homeless, each of these categories receives less pay, value, acclaim, validation and support for their work and wisdom. As Life Artists to this process, we worked with the personal lineage of our own hearts and the ways we've learned to be in relationship with the creative nature of our being and inherent voice. This is how we heal through life's sacred alchemy.

As each *Faces of the Mother* Artist committed to and held her value and purpose within her own being, she allowed a reorientation to occur. Here she was directly initiated by her inherent design that is based in union. This shed new light and possibility on what might be possible through her. As our process moved along and each of the Life Artists worked with attuning to her Mother Face, she became its living voice and expression.

Mothering Soul Fertility

I was initiated into the deepest workings of creation through becoming a mother. This book and ensuing journey is my eternal thanks for this path.

Many are surprised to hear I never intended to get married or have children. And like many things in my life, I entered mothering, relationship and family resisting. My masculine nature and the protective inclinations I carry to safeguard the Sacred Feminine, run strong and deep in my blood and convictions. I was terrified of becoming a mother. How was I going to protect my own innocence and feminine nature through a path (mothering and family life) that the current societal conditions were doing little to safeguard, honor or validate the feminine through?

Taking the long-term experiences from my own mothering and fertility journey, and engaging with the *Faces of the Mother* process, helped me move from an inherent pattern of resistance and being overly protective, into a vast softening, ultimately trusting and becoming Her face, breath and heart. The very innocence of Her.

As I surrendered into the path of mothering my children, I discovered a limitless storehouse of primordial wisdom that rocked my world and filled me with the fluidity of creation. I learned that the richness of who we are and are inherently designed to be lives within our being. It is found in the bellies of ourselves. This is where the map of our soul unfolding is stored. As we learn to engage with and trust this, we bring the richest creativity of nature forth. This is our soul fertility.

Our soul fertility is the organic way we are designed from within the intimate recesses of creation. This is how we connect to our purpose, divine human design, and the interrelationship we carry with all life. This is what whispers through our DNA and reveals in how we show up to life, and how life shows up through us. Our soul fertility pulses within our blood and bones. It flows through our womb and organs. It can be touched through our skin as it absorbs into our muscle and tissues, and flows out from it. This is the organic makeup of our fullest human experience and expression. And it's more tangible than anything gets!

Here we reach the place within that's never been touched by an outside or separate world. We discover our deepest faith in what it means to be, share and express who we authentically are. In the recesses of our creative soul fertility we make love with God, by whatever name we call out to the source of our lives. Here we see with our own eyes how the sacred and earthly join together inside of us. We touch our sexual and soulful nature and realize they are one and the same! Within our soul fertility our deepest creations come to life. And we allow ourselves to naturally unfold through them and they through us. The untouched place within comes into focus and we let this vast empty darkness of our being be the floorboard for our eternal and external existence.

This is our inherent soul fertility. This is what *Faces of the Mother* was built upon. This framework supported each woman to return to the untouched place within, through a natural clearing and rebuilding, so she could feel and create an authentic expression of herself and the Mother as one, birthing and breathing each other into existence.

Trusting Impulse

Maybe I'm just getting older. And maybe I'm maturing, surrendering more, or simply being more true to who I am. Whatever the comprising factors, through *Faces of the Mother* I realized, and began to trust, how my authentic and enduring creativity arises on sacred impulse.

This doesn't mean I don't plan, or reflect on my vision and set intentions. This is about how when something is ripe, ready and here, I feel and greet it, following its guidance in innocent wonder. I listen and show up, asking life to reveal a pathway. And then I feel what is coming forward, greeting this in mutual knowing. I am working with something beyond what I can name, form or even put a face or label to. Quite simply all I can do is enter like a child and remain open to play. When I do this, creation is fluid and alive. It is inter-dynamic and mutually engaging. And I may not get it or even believe it is 'right'. This is a process not housed in the mind. It is a full body exploration. Something is being created in the moment and also being listened to, drawing forth and out from its ancestry and original source. This is essential to my process and to what occurred here. This is what the artistry of the feminine is all about... feeling each step in active relating and co-creating.

I have come to see that such impulses are the direct internal experience of our co-creative system proclaiming, "Now is the time. Go ahead." It makes me think of the story of the little angel standing over each blade of grass whispering, "Grow, grow! It's time." Our inner impulse reveals the way creation *actually* and uniquely works through us. It is the resounding song of the vast mystery we each can and are touching, listening and responding to with our whole being.

And so it was with *Faces of the Mother*. It had an unfolding... it began with a preconception and inception. The inception was comprised of many things coming together, engaging with and interrelating. I have no doubt the women who've journeyed with me in the intimate pathways of this project were a part of its initial conception before I knew them and what would occur.

Creation happens in ways beyond what our everyday eyes can see, though we are personally and collectively strengthening this muscle more. What the deeper throes of our souls can feel, sense and experience is where creation slips through the cracks into embodiment and form. This is where *Faces of the Mother* found its structure and intent.

Many of our Artists expressed this realization throughout our process... that our connection to love can only be spoken of and shared in glimpses. This project is but a small fraction of what we are actively engaged in as a living humanity *all the time*. Indeed it is a small fraction. As each of us offers up our fraction, the whole begins to be revealed and to shine evermore brightly.

It takes every one of us to rise and proclaim the truth about our selves and holy existence. And it takes but one to believe in and move forth along the way. *Faces of the Mother* is an offering towards this. Through our capacity to follow an inner impulse, something grand is occurring, being revealed and co-created. As I look through these pages and as I've sat with these Feminine Life Artists, this almost imperceptible expression of something vast and encompassing causes me to no longer doubt our purpose and impact. What we feel cannot be denied.

It was all I had to go on in the beginning. It is what, even now, I can only trust.

Preconception

Beloved Mother Father God, Divine Creation

I call out to you, humbly and innocently, wounded and in my healing. I call out on behalf of these women and all they are connected to. I call out on behalf of myself, and all that I am connected to. Please watch over us. Please guide us beyond ways we've ever known what guidance was. Help us to be true to our-selves. And more so, to be true to the life of the Feminine within, knowing when we're true to the Feminine, we're true to all and all things. Please help us in ways we didn't even know we were longing for help with. And help us to see ourselves in the way you, precious creation and creator, see us. With eyes of the one that birthed us, with the knowing that held us in sacred holiness as we were being crafted and created for a life and purpose that was unique and so needed for the entire world. And indeed in the places we've forgotten, but more so from the places that we remember, help us continue to fortify and strengthen so every aspect of this journey, every aspect of our togetherness and our own unique expression, will be fluidly formed as if we're simply being kissed by the grace of the Mother. That softness, and also that ferocity, will never desert us or leave us alone, but will remind us we are beautiful, and we are so loved. We are worthy, and we are Her daughters. Please bless these artists and myself. Bless our families, homes, our animals, and all we call community and precious to us. Bless us for this time together over the next 3 months with the rising and falling of the moon, and the creations and expressions that come forth. Bless us manifold to continue to refine our purpose and our knowing, so we may each be like shooting stars dropping upon the earth in the exact location to ripple out and magnify the greatest awareness of the cosmos.

~ FROM *FACES OF THE MOTHER*, A PRAYER OF WELCOMING

ଔ

I often find it hard to distinguish the details of how it all begins. For me, preconception usually comes when all else has fallen away and there is nothing more to grasp onto or long for. It arises when I am in my deepest surrender. Out of this allowance what I could never imagine begins to form. Within the darkness beyond what I can see, something is restored. A light flicks on. I realize I've been resting in the vast unknowingness. And I am not alone. It is here I experience my life's recommitment to itself.

I've come to experience this restoration as something always underway. As I look over the course of my life, I see that as things were being stripped bare, restoration was an integral aspect of its intention and process. Like the inner realms of a woman's body preparing for menstruation, the lining of her uterus washes clean with blood to prepare an inner space for the fertilization of new possibility. Hand-in-hand death, transition and rebirth co-exist in a primordial place I call preconception. It is the ground of surrender into who we have always been. It is the restoration of our self in harmony and union.

During late summer 2010, I conceived my third child. This hallmarked a return into the core of my being as my past collided with all possible futures. I greeted wounding of my soul, family lineage patterns, financial dissolution, and letting go of everything I thought I'd be doing. The chaos and tenderness were imminent at every turn. I learned to show up to the present and my own presence, and to let that be enough.

That winter I took a course entitled, "Soulful Women," with Devaa Haley Mitchell and Elaine Doughty [1], based on the 13 Moon Mystery School brought forth through Ariel Spilsbury, a wise elder and creator of the *Sanctuary of the Open Heart* [2]. Engaging with this material alongside the initiation and healing that organically accompanies pregnancy, I entered a vast and primordial reorientation to the essence of my nature... to the creative passage through my being and life.

Through pregnancy a woman is held by the power of the Mother. A new layer of surrender is beckoned with each conception, trimester, with each birth, adoption and mothering transition. In this pregnancy I entered a threshold of welcoming the fullness of the Mother's uncontainable force through me. The past 15 years of my work and mothering had been dedicated to exploring the landscape of feminine wisdom. Now I could only fall to my knees and humbly greet the ways I'd feared, been denying, distrusting and devaluing the not-so-comfortable, unknowable, all powerful and indefinable qualities of Her within.

I began to look at where I'd disconnected from love. I embraced how frightened I was of what She might look like or create through me. I cried tears of remorse for how I believed this power couldn't be contained in my own body, or through my relating. I wiped each tear away as I discovered She and I were one. My name was Hers. My breath and breasts, my belly and being, were the vessel for the vast creation and power of the feminine. This was growing as a physical and rooted experience through myself.

---

1   Soulful Women program (now entitled, 'The Feminine Alchemy Immersion') - http://soulfulwomencourses.com/Certificate

2   Sanctuary of the Open Heart - www.13moonmysteryschool.org

I accepted that I had run from being consumed by that which lives in the vastness of what I may never know, yet is experienced each day and moment through my innocence, vulnerability and presence. I grasped, released, gasped and then simply allowed myself to be refashioned through the restoration that had always been underway.

I discovered a place where running was no longer an option, and chose to use my remaining time in pregnancy to rest in Her force living through me unhindered. I often heard the guidance and began to trust it, "Learn to rest in this darkness and no longer seek for or turn on a light."

This was not an easy or comfortable commitment, especially for one who had wanted to live in the "lightness" and peace of her soul. I was now learning to allow any perception I held to be embraced in tenderness. I was being fashioned as the peace that no longer would choose to separate my light from my darkness... to separate any aspect of myself from Her.

I developed a blood clot early in this pregnancy and discovered I had a genetic condition inherited from my father. For 9 months into postpartum, I chose to pursue medical treatment by injecting blood thinner into my growing belly, into the container of life for my precious growing babe. The medical risks were considered life threatening if I did not tend the clot throughout the pregnancy. I was often treated as having a life or death condition, and was turned away by midwives for care. I ended up turning from the care that didn't support my home birth decision against all medical advice, and learned to determinedly and in surrender follow the soul of my babe's and our unified guidance. I was left in awe with no translation for any of it. I let the Mother embrace me and clung to this like a lost girl.

Through this journey I faced layers of pigeonholing my existence... looking at how I was willing to allow only *certain* aspects or components of myself forth as they aligned with what was acceptable and comfortable to others, or to what I had understood as appropriate based on my childhood. I hadn't trusted the Mother to love me completely, and hadn't fully believed in myself to live this. Even though the work of the Sacred Feminine was where I'd devoted my energies, I was now experiencing the deepest roots of devaluation of the full feminine and how it had taken hold. In entering the wisdom of the 13 Moon Mystery School,

I welcomed the archetypes of the alchemical Feminine to support opening a greater passage into the coherency of these inner workings and my wholeness.

As I ripened with child and the wisdom of the Mother, I opened to the many faces of Her. I was developing a fullness for myself and all of creation. In Her incomprehensible expression and embrace, I devoted my heart and womb to creating passage for love to be welcomed and intimately made known through me.

Inception

Three years later in the late spring of 2013, I felt a stirring inside. It felt ancient, as if everything I had lived for was colliding into a moment of crescendo. It felt like something was rising up and being born. It was indefinable and too familiar a feeling.

I had turned 42 near the spring equinox that year. At that time I began a 9-month intensive training into the landscape of Sacred Sexual Union with Anaiya Sophia, a mystical enchantress living in Southern France.[1] Here I faced my deepest wounds as I cradled parts of me that still believed something outside and separate was at the helm of my fertility... of my creative process, choices and life's expression.

To enter this journey of Sacred Union I'd consciously made a commitment to look at all the ways I was holding back, creating blockades in my direct communion with source, and engaging in behaviors that supported me *not* loving myself, family, partner and life with everything I had. Though this felt like a tall order, it was the only purpose I had before me as the past years stripped any other reason for living away. As they say, "the choice was simple."

With the blossoming of the earth's springtime around me, a natural mirroring enfolded within. Reaching out through a newsletter to my community I offered an invitation, welcoming co-journeyers into the landscape I knew intimately, into the world of the Sacred Feminine... into the heart of the Mother.

I drew upon the structure of a series I'd shared the previous year, offering mothers an opportunity to engage with alchemical expressions of the Mother

---

1   Anaiya Sophia - http://anaiyasophia.com/

through dialogue, inner wisdom and sacred activities. I had called this series, "Faces of the Mother... reclaiming the wisdom, power and essence of motherhood." I was inspired to draw upon this original foundation sensing a rich possibility for personal and societal feminine restoration. I wanted to explore how to unquestionably come alive with the Mother and share this with others. I wanted to live into the guidance. She'd offered through my life, creating opportunities for women to deeply know themselves as Life Artists imbued with the potential of their Soul Fertility. It had been my intent through my work to share this. Now I wanted to travel all the way, leaving no stone unturned or corner untended. Leaving nothing unnoticed or in the dark bellows to feel unloved.

An invitation was sent forth...

> *I call to you from the depths of our womb and soul... please join me in this expressive journey into the realms of our vital feminine creation. I am bringing together a transformative collection of feminine wisdom, courage and power, to inspire and support all women and mothers. My intent is to impact, demonstrate and revitalize the inner knowing, validity and sacred expression of the essence of our Mother Wisdom. Our culture has forgotten the deep wealth and wisdom of the Mother. It is time to remember... The Mother is the original starting point. Through Her all things take form in perfect time. We are the original starting point. Through us all things take form in perfect time.*

~ *FACES OF THE MOTHER*, INITIAL COMMUNITY INVITATION

ॐ

Sacred Process

I was startled by the purposeful conviction arising in connection to this invitation. It felt invincible, like nothing would get in its way. And it also felt soft and downy, like a malleable fluidity that had no need to protect, control or watch over anything. I was clear of the project's intent...

> *This is a personal transformative journey and a powerful intentioned collaboration to impact the world and way we've expressed the wisdom of our feminine essence and creativity. My background is in bringing women together through sacred purpose, honoring the gift and power of the collective and individual in unity. Each artist will be cherished... her sense of herself recreated for all time. By accessing and playing with archetypical expressions of feminine wisdom and power, we awaken and honor our own multi-faceted gifts. The many faces of the mother are our own.*

~ FACES OF THE MOTHER, INITIAL COMMUNITY INVITATION

CR

I longed to support women... to aid in the intimate and lasting realizations that propel one unequivocally into their inner wisdom and direct creative connection. It was what I wished to give and serve. I wanted to understand why many women I knew and had worked with, including myself, were not feeling love's encapsulation, guidance and support at every turn. Since childhood I had a clear knowing of the love I came from, yet doubt and self-denial were ever present. I wanted to commit to my soul fully and knew from my work and experience in the depths of the Sacred Feminine that this was going to be a collaborative adventure. If we wanted to enter the landscape of the Mother we would enter through the place where we come together as one.

Inspired by the 13 archetypes of Ariel Spilsbury's 13 Moon Mystery School, and the natural awakenings that ensued in the after-birth of my third child, I prayed for and called upon a renewed relationship with the many facets of the Mother. With each stage of life I had an opportunity to greet new and ancient parts of myself. During the three years after my third son's conception, I felt into these archetypal powers, asking them to guide me into terrain I'd been avoiding, had once known deeply, resonated naturally with now, and wanted to explore evermore. I awakened to the depth of the Mother through my 15 years of mothering and was ready to face the ways I'd disproportioned Her through my misconceptions, and from being raised in a culture that overtly Christianized and downplayed the inherent power I had touched the moment new life arose in my womb.

I organically turned to the Divine Mother for guidance since childhood. Now I was learning to trust in creation more than ever before. I wanted to reveal and rely upon an intimate embodied experience of this uncontainable wisdom. I wanted to feel that Her love was real, to touch and taste an unshakable faith in who I am and who we can be together.

As I followed this inner prayer into a softening form and framework, I felt 13 faces reveal. It was these I relied upon to show me the way through the *Faces of the Mother* process.[1] I sensed that in connecting participants with these archetypal powers, inviting them in to their own relating and self expression, a transformation would result in the way we'd prior engaged with and permitted our feminine worth and wisdom to shine.

I've always carried the sense we are in this together. We are living for something that cannot be known through one of us; it is meant to be experienced through all. I've naturally gravitated towards drawing people together to understand something in myself, to watch and listen as life reflects a collaborative reality. The *Faces of the Mother* process followed these natural inclinations. The wisdom revealed that for Her to be authentically expressed it would take more than just me. It would take us working together as We.

In my initial community invitation I welcomed up to 13 Feminine Life Artists to join in this collaboration. A general overview was shared and an invitation to feel into which Mother Face(s) most appealed to each artist. A rhythm of creative expression was anchored following the waxing and waning of the moon, and an authentic look at one's own commitment to self was established.

---

1   the initial inspiration for these 13 Faces is shared about in "A Bit About Archetypes," p. 61

I knew the lens of this project would peer into the ways the feminine had been denied in our culture and selves. It would be essential that participants were honest as they were committing to themselves and their source connection above all else, committing to their inherent value and creative expression. This was the touchstone we would come back to again and again as a million resistances showed their face.

At the onset I offered a loose vision of what I wished to create: a book of the 13 Faces of the Mother. I partnered women with 1 face each, and 2 artists had 2, of the archetypal Mother Faces.

- Each artist will be selected and connected to 1 or more of the following aspects of Mother Wisdom: Mystic, Artist, Healer, Distiller, Decomposer, Midwife, Creatress, Leader, Regenerator, Priestess, Bestower, Beloved, and the 13th is a compilation of these Unified. These are called the 'Mother Faces'.

- Artists will connect with and inwardly listen to the wisdom of these Mother Faces to create an artistic expression(s).

- Selected artists will receive empowerment and support during a 3-month creative wombing journey.

- The final Faces of the Mother collection will be a version of the 13 expressions of our Mother Wisdom through poetry, guided inspiration, sacred medicine, transformational processes, personal exploration and artists' artwork.

With that written invitation I shared a beckoning from my heart, recognition to those Feminine Life Artists who were deeply drawn to this collaboration. I knew this process reflected the inter-dynamic nature of life actively at play. I knew I was calling in and being called upon by co-journeyers who shared the same intent and longing for this grand adventure from inside their own being, carrying it beyond time and space into this moment together.

The below audio recording was shared with my initial written invitation...

Good morning and sacred full moon blessings.

I'm sitting outside right now and the rain is coming down, as it's the morning of the full moon right after our summer solstice.

I feel such a sense of homecoming, serenity and stillness. I wanted to voice my invitation to this upcoming sacred project that I feel has been brewing inside me for so long. And I feel the artists who come forward to join in this creative collaboration feel the same... that this seed of longing to express that deeper wisdom from inside of us in a way that is beautiful and feminine, strong, soft and courageous, is also felt deeply, clearly, personally and with conviction at this time.

In the past few days such sweetness, clarity, such stripping away has occurred so that now there's a simplicity of what I long to do. And I invite you to join me in that simplicity of being who we are together.

As I feel the rain now upon my skin, and I look upon the flowers and hear the birds, I share that this invitation really comes from that. It comes from my experience of life and how life grows. Truly how life grows. Not a forced manipulation of how I think or we have thought life grows, but a deep honor, watching and witnessing that I feel blessed my spirit has guided me in. And I know your spirit has guided you in to.

The invitation is to be a part of the upcoming creation of the Faces of the Mother collection. In the past few months I've gone through a lot of stripping away, and looking more deeply at how can I move forward with my gifts. I know you have as well. That has lead me to realize how important it is to stand strong and true, and put forth in ever expanding, more poignant ways, more ever-accessible ways, the gift, the light and the power that lives inside of me, and lives inside all women...

Many blessings upon this full moon and upon your journey, and upon whatever you choose in connection to this invitation. I love you so dearly, and I know *life loves you so passionately, and is always guiding you to exactly what is best for your sacred seed unfolding. Om Shanti.*

~ *FACES OF THE MOTHER*, FULL MOON INITIAL AUDIO INVITATION

CR

Wilderness Within

When planning for an adventure one cannot fully know the experience she will have or where she'll end up. At the onset of this process I could not have planned for the full course or prepared for the seemingly off-road destinations we would visit. Each step and side-step brought us deeply into what each woman most wished for... to learn, see and experience for herself, unbeknownst to me and my original intention. This is the ultimate path of Soul Fertility and Feminine Life Artistry. This is our surrender into pure and unbridled trust in creation itself. I knew this pathway was in the hands of each Life Artist's connection to the Mother and my ever-deepening surrender into this guidance.

For this adventure I trusted in my inner wisdom and sacred medicine tools to support where and when needed. Each of the Life Artists would have her own unique process based on where she was coming from and where she was longing to go. Each of these Feminine Creators would move through this journey in her own style and rhythm, based on her soul's guidance and creativity. I turned to the Mother in prayer and simply proclaimed, "Show us the way."

11 women, including myself, set off on the full moon of July 22, 2013, Mary Magdalene's feast day. We opened a pathway asking to come to the center of ourselves to resurrect guidance and feel into relationship with the power and presence of the Mother. The path was initiated through an email and audio welcoming. I took a trip to the beach to consecrate our journey, offering a prayer and each woman's name to the ocean and earth, into the Great Mother's care.

Welcome to Faces of the Mother.

I feel so deeply touched to be beginning this journey and to be anchoring in with each of you.

I was at the beach, at the Oregon Coast, this past weekend and am just returning and integrating. On one of the mornings I headed out for my ritual of time to myself, walking on the beach before anyone else is awake. Getting to be there in that solitude also filled with such immense presence. I carried each of you, literally in my pocket (laughing), and also in my heart. I thought I would send your names into the ocean. And I did upon a prayer. I thought I'd also throw your names out upon slips of paper, sending them onto the waves, knowing ultimately that is the greatest gift. When we begin an adventure we anchor into surrender. Surrender in a way that we know we are not separate, we are not alone. We are not surrendering into something that is different or separate from us. We are surrendering into the greatest fullness of who we are and who we are together.

I was surprised when the guidance shifted. Instead of placing your names onto the water, I was guided to bury them. And bury them deep in this red, rich, sandy, wet earth that had dunes people had been carving their names into and lovers writing, "Becky and Matt together forever" on. The spot I was drawn to bury our names, the names of each of the Life Artists of the Faces of the Mother Collection, was under this little sand enclave mound that simply said,

"I love you."

I put our names on slips of paper there, and covered it with a sprinkling of sand and a rock and some dried leaf petals from a bouquet my husband had given me a few months ago. With that I said a prayer, which on some level I ask to come forward now so I can speak that and we can each hear and hold that together as we continue forward on this journey of creation...

~ *Faces of the Mother*, FULL MOON OPENING AND WELCOMING

☙

A week after we began our journey, another woman came forward with interest in participating. At that point all the Mother Faces had been partnered with an artist except for one, the Mother as Unifier – the expression of the faces together as one. I invited this woman to feel into her resonance with that. After personal reflection she came onboard making us 12. Later this same woman would fall away as we came to the end of our creative collaboration, bringing us back to 11. Without knowing this would be the path or end result, this woman's participation provided a powerful opening for our final expression as we each deeply rooted in to the depth of true unification.

Rhythm of the Moon – Rhythm of the Season

One of the cornerstones we drew upon and invested in through this process was a trust and reliance on our relationship with nature... with the moon and earth, and with our bodies and seasons. As we enter this inner-outer feminine terrain, we are welcomed and in alliance with the wisdom of the celestial cosmos and organic matter of the earth.

This journey began in the weeks after summer's solstice. At this time I had been working with the rhythms of spring's internal ripening, and now offered its vision seed into the care of the sun, earth, water and air, and into the hands of this collaboration of women. Our process officially ended near the turn of autumn, as we closed down our active journey together. This was a natural time for inward harvesting and celebration of soul growth, reflected by nature's harvest and inward preparations for winter all around. All the artists' material was turned in to me by winter's solstice. This supported my drawing in and resting at the center of the nourishment we had harvested. With the turn of autumn into winter, I let go of guiding our collective energy and moved inward to work with my creative fertility and compiling this book.

As these larger seasonal transitions held the cornerstones of our *Faces of the Mother* process, the internal transitions flowed through the rhythmic cycles of the moon. As we entered new moons we drew inward to explore where we had traveled over the past month and what had moved through us, opening to what was newly arising and ready to come forth. Our touchstone dates were on the new moons. This was the stage in our process when I asked how each Life Artist was doing and requested a snapshot of where she was in time/space.

As we drew towards full moons, we entered the landscape of our Creative Support Wombings, breathing into and through the wisdom of our soul and fertility, into our inherent sustenance to forge a pathway for the next unfolding layer of our Mother Face expression to form. Creative Support Wombings were an intuitively guided audio journey to support each artist in her Soul Fertility, and to celebrate where we were collectively in the vast support of the Mother's Womb. We leaned into and listened to the cycles of our lives and bodies, to our blood and where we were at in the evolution of our womanhood and feminine expression.

Gazing at the moon is testament to the wisdom coming forth through *Faces of the Mother*. The many cycles, expressions and power of what we hold within us is revealed through the Feminine Life Artists' words and creations. In tapping into this ancient legacy and primordial wisdom through nature's creative cycles, we are carried through the valleys of our feminine restoration, revitalizing and calling Her face forth through our own breath and body into form.

Support Wombings & Touchstones

During this intentioned 3-month process, 4 Creative Support Wombings were offered as audio recordings on the full moons. The intent of these was to provide support for each woman to feel into her direct relationship with the Womb of Life and Great Mother, naturally offering awareness of our sustained creativity and Soul Fertility flourishing.

These Wombings offered an intimate connection between myself, each artist and us all. The transmission of my voice and the energy of my heart and soul, supported us feeling into the living, breathing, interrelated, co-creative experience we were undergoing that was alive and also birthing amongst us at the same time.

Four Touchstone dates were set on the new moons. These were opportunities to check in with oneself and reflect on where you were, if you were honoring your commitment, and what was arising through you. Artists sent brief emails, offered pictures of their work thus far, shared poems, texted messages, and remained silent through these times.

After each Touchstone I was drawn to create snapshots of where each woman shared she was in the process so we could feel into the collaborative nature of this project and what was coming forth. I wanted to reveal what was real, what I was seeing and we were creating, what was coming alive and being birthed. Through this I sensed we would richly understand and directly know the ever-present collaborative nature of not just this project, but also of our world and lives. I was living in trust of our synergy, and offered these reflections in celebration of what was more real than anything else... our togetherness in creation creating.

Here is our first Touchstone Co-Creation... a collaborative poem from our Feminine Life Artists. Words, sentences, bits and statements from each woman's sharing were woven together to offer this sacred expression of how She was coming alive through us all.[1]

---

1 To listen to an audio recording of our first Touchstone Co-Creation, visit my website: http://www. sharonannrose.com/videos—audios. You will find it listed under: *Faces of the Mother*: a creative support wombing

Fertile Listening

Today, sitting down to check in, I am here.
It is a tender season for me,
This shedding could not have happened at a better time.
It may be a touchstone day but I am beginning to
experience this as something of a lifeline.
I trust this process. I sense it is happening already.
"Lean in" I hear again and truly need.
I'm terrified.
Deep, pretty much in my pelvis.
Mutual deepest honor and precious humility,
I know she will be found. She must.
What if I was allowed to just go. Go and be. Who I am. If there was no doubt,
no questioning, no worry or fear, no negative voices or shame. What if I were
totally accepted, as is, and my work in the world, whatever it is, were wanted,
needed, embraced. If I magically had the ability to just be – my pleasure,
my dreams, and spirit – what then?   What would my work be?
A very present and meditative process. I have been coming to it again and again,
facing my challenges to make both space and time to create.
Packing some art supplies, enjoying the beautiful ocean and the
feeling that comes with being present in Mother Nature.
Leaving myself open for other possibilities to float in,
I am thrilled by it.
Embracing myself and initiating myself as a priestess of the mother.
You can wrap your arms around the collective daughters of this world
and let them know their true beauty is more than skin deep.

How and
where do I
shine my
Light ?

How and where do I also
engage and embrace my
Shadow?

Snapshots of those moments of grace, corner of the eye. Texture, soft and
beautiful. Rough, funny, sad, bright, low light, foggy. Always present.

I pray for our imagination to release every condition that forms
a barrier between our selves and God and Goddess. May we
proceed into these moments of opening an attunement to keenly
listen to what is not real any longer... From here this turn of new
perspective is a beginning, rising and setting and wish arrived.
So great to hear about Jacinda joining in.

Welcome Jacinda ;-)

The Sacred Artist.

~ FACES OF THE MOTHER TEAM, OUR TOUCHSTONE COLLABORATION

ᘓ

Though some of the women knew one another beforehand, most did not. The
Touchstones were opportunities to glimpse the nature of each woman's soul
and our unified connection. After Touchstone Co-Creations were shared, artists commented that what another woman said could have been her own words.
Each expression conveyed her deepest inner experience. Our human faces, not
yet revealed, had already fallen away. We were entering this landscape, walking
heart-to-heart and soul-to-soul. Nameless and faceless, learning to live and be
the essence of who we are. I was struck by how quickly our voices were breathing,

weaving, living, acting and expressing as one. Sacred sisterhood was alive amongst us and needed nothing from me to be facilitated, formed and present.

From the onset I sensed we would not be spending time on personal introductions or getting to know one another beforehand. The deeper intent of this journey was to feel into the unbreakable and eternal connection that is naturally here as we come together in sacred space and co-create for a unified purpose. There was nothing I needed to do to draw these women together. Through their commitment to themselves and to the love of the Mother revealing, we were seeing we already were sisters... growing into a container of family. This is what emerges when we are in our deepest presence.

From Our Life Artists

Since this was a process about embodiment and direct experience, it is hard to convey and even harder to find words to describe what actually occurred for and within each woman. This journey was deeply personal and unique to each Life Artist, while also richly revealing how our experiences mirror one another's and the collective experience of life.

As Life Artists made their way through the *Faces of the Mother* journey, I asked for their feedback and reflections. Here is what they experienced in their own words and how they would describe our creative process to a friend:

> Roller coaster, funhouse, mind boggling, interplanetary, really fucking hard, and meeting 12 new allies I may never meet – all of whom are midwives. The process came in the midst of some enormous and difficult changes in my life. It's a little hard to separate things out still, but I know that I'm grateful to have had something to come back to again and again, that had clear deadlines, and inspirations for creativity. It helped immensely to put myself on a schedule and muddle through trying to express things artistically. I don't think I would have been making anything except tears, otherwise. ~ Mystic

CR

I have been holding this project and process so close to my heart, so as I think about describing it to a friend, I'm still a bit lost for words. I might start by saying I'm part of a group of women artists that have agreed to be led on a journey together in spirit to find the face/essence of the mother that is inside each of us. We've agreed to experience her, live and breathe her, and bottle some of her up to recreate her in our own perfect image. And then share her with ourselves and the world. ~ Healer

❧

A powerful process that is individual and yet collaborative through a spiritual connection. It is private and yet shared through the knowing of other women doing the same work. ~ Distiller

❧

Whew! Heavy. Hard. Wonderful. Painful. Recommended. ~ Decomposer

❧

I've had a lot of confusion about the goal of myself, and I had to really delve down deep through the tears to get at the gem inside my soul. In order to really connect with others, you can't just pretend it's happening, you have to WORK at it – take TIME to sit and connect... LISTEN... allow your heart to OPEN. It's like riding a roller-coaster. Sometimes you're bored, sometimes your head is RUSHING to keep up with your body (or vice versa) and sometimes you wonder oh WHY did I get on this ride in the first place? Until you get to the end, and the adrenaline is so wonderful, as you're getting off the ride you say, THAT'S IT. I'M GOING AGAIN! I am growing and loving my growth. I have carved out time for my creative self outside of my home and my regular activities and it is enriching me greatly. Working in conjunction with these other women is very powerful. Kind of weird. I felt like they were urging me on in my work, even though we had never talked, nor met face to face. ~ Midwife

❧

The 13 Faces of Mother initiative, for me, has been about exploring one's creative potential and relationship to the Divine. It has been a most intimate exploration of Self and the creative process. In some ways it is an individual journey (it is self-paced, in the privacy of one's home and immersed in one's own life situations), yet the interconnectedness of being part of a larger purpose, receiving group reflections and orienting to common milestones (dates and touchstones) provides grounding support and a foundational framework. A sacred time and space is created. It has certainly helped me extend my experience beyond what I know I am able to do alone. ~ Leader

⟋⟍

I would describe this to a friend that it has been quite an odd and wonderful journey. I would tell them of the deep intention of not only Sharon Ann Rose, but of all the faceless women involved in this project, for though I haven't met most of them, I was aware of them within their own journeys towards this one big movement together. And we will come together whether we ever see each other or not, because the intention, the support and energy were real and present throughout the project. I did talk to a friend about it. It was like describing a new relationship in which I was involved; and as it grew deeper, through the wonder and discomfort of it all, there emerged an ever-growing seed. ~ Regenerator

⟋⟍

It's all about reaching deep inside and bringing out that something... creatively. ~ Priestess

⟋⟍

It's a bit tricky but I keep trying. Whatever I say seems to barely touch it. Some part of me feels fledgling, like what is beginning to open must be tended or it can shut again too easily. Part of that may be in using fewer words. Perhaps not attempting to talk about it too soon. Like with incubating fledgling creative ideas. ~ Bestower & Beloved

Sacred Collaboration

The beauty of this process revealed what I'd sensed, yet hadn't fully trusted to be real or enduring around me. The layers of protection we erect around our hearts and uphold throughout our lives can keep us from living the truth we carry.

Our *Faces of the Mother* collection is a testament to the sacred collaboration of life... to the reality that what lives within is also surrounding us. In our hearts, wombs, bellies, intuition and souls we know we are interconnected and mutually interdependent. We can sense our lives are based upon and supported by this. We are living for a common and unified purpose. As one of our Life Artists stated, *"...for though I haven't met most of them (the other artists), I was aware of them within their own journeys towards this one big movement together."* This depicts the reality we share with all of humanity. We are in this together, moving towards one big movement and common unified purpose, whether we meet or not, whether we know it or not.

Yet where do we look in our culture, society, in our institutions and news to see this truth revealed? We are shown through a multitude of ways we are divided, moving towards unique, distinct and separate goals. And on one level we are. Yet what happens when we travel deeper within ourselves? When we go to these recesses within to feel, see and personally connect with our interrelational humanity? To live in and through any felt sense of unified purpose, we trust we are connected to the same thing and source. We trust that all we do and share from these inner promptings is somehow interrelated to what will serve all others.

This is how we anchored in to our personal piece and collective purpose throughout our journey. So let us begin here with you. And from this moment forth, let us begin here with all. Beginning through these steps we've taken in rooted faith and feminine impulse, we choose to follow something far richer than any one of us has ever been told, yet every one of us has known and cherished deep within.

The *Faces of the Mother* journey was inspired through sacred collaboration. I knew that in my own life all I've lived through has been collaborating to draw me into the next moment. Every person I've met, teacher I've sat with, every experience I've encountered, confusion and heartache I've held, every babe and creation that formed and birthed through my body, has carried me into the beckoning of what came forth next. Every plant, creature, energy, nothingness, voice, story and season has woven together to support this out breath. And so it has been with each of the Life Artists who came forth to travel this journey with me. And now it is with you.

We are never alone. We will always be in this together.

As we allow and accept this truth, sacred kin begin to reveal, showing their true form and formless face. Standing by our side in expression of what is ever present within us all.

Into the Root Feminine

To complete their creative offerings, each Artist leaned into and faced her own ancestry, drawing on guidance from and letting go of patterns from her mother, grandmothers, great grandmothers, general "Mother culture", spiritual Mother and Mother self. This was not formed or guided from the outside. It is what naturally awakened through our journey, prompted by each woman's internal process. Through the inherent scope of our creative work and intentions, each woman was drawn to where she believed she came from, naturally falling into the arms of a unified love that birthed her far beyond that.

To enter her root feminine, each Artist looked at how she'd been showing up, saying yes or no to her inner wellspring of creativity. This allowed her to explore the ground of her artistic self-conception, birth and childhood, sensing how these seasons in her life and their inherent messages impacted her ability to bring forth her current creativity, power and union. This resulted in finding and forging a new pathway for each woman to grapple with and claim her own freedom, learning to love herself even through her greatest fear. Life Artists discovered the Feminine face of God as their own.

This journey and what was formed arose through the primordial places within all women, where we intuitively know and can touch the inner feminine power we contain to birth life through our self-love, cherishing its inherent and priceless value.

Incomprehensibility

As we neared our second Touchstone cycle, more than mid-way through our 3-month journey, things heated up. Major crisis were occurring in the lives of almost every Feminine Life Artist. What these women were now asking of themselves had reached all-out proportions. Ultimately, many came to see their situation as being crafted up so they could discover how deeply they were willing to stand in and for themselves and their inherent value. Through these challenges, each woman proclaimed what it is she longed for above all else.

During this alchemical time, one Artist developed kidney stones and let go of a long-term relationship. Another released her house to foreclosure. Another came home to a contained oven fire in her kitchen, resulting in excessive smoke damage. She and her family moved 5 times in 6 weeks while their house was cleaned and kitchen repaired. On and on it went. The fires of our Mother Faces ignited, burned and died down. And each woman's initiation into the cauldron of her creativity heightened.

What these women faced was incomprehensible. What they allowed to come forth was monumental. What they kept committing to was indestructible. Over and over they reinvested in their resounding Yes! to life and their willingness to create through the fires, through their capability to forge forth and onward, digging ever deeper into the possibility of what was awakening and birthing through us all.

As I looked at this vast and barren landscape, at what appeared as desolation and destruction, into the heart wrenching transitions so many of these women now faced, I opened my heart in prayer. I surrendered again to this process. I honored my own healing, moving out of patterns of trying to keep everyone and everything safe and comfortable. I claimed a deeper trust in what was *actually* happening. Its impact was beyond what I could see or may ever know. This was my commitment... to the Mother and the alchemical container provided for our transformation. I opened my arms wide to what would be born through this experience, even as my own self was burning away.

Burning Embers

The fires burned steady and revealed through our next Touchstone date and check-in. At this stage most of the women had 'stalled' in their creative process, facing external situations that consumed their attention and internal patterns that felt larger than life. Many of the Artists were working with deep childhood wounds and core default patterns arising through their bodies, life's manifestation and close relationships.

The Touchstone date was for personal and collective grounding. The expressions from each Artist were shockingly similar, containing elements of exhaustion, letting go and deep surrender. Things were falling away at a rapid pace – old notions and concepts no longer held. Artwork was transforming, vision reforming. Friendships and relationships dying. Understandings of true home finding their source inside oneself.

Through my witnessing of this process, while also being an integral part, I again shared a collective snapshot with the women of the depth, heartache and opening that was occurring for and through us. For many the exposure of these tender vulnerabilities brought intense fear and a desire to shut down or run away. Yet somehow each woman found her way through this veil being lifted, discovering within our collective that she *was* safe to be who she was. Old masks and hardened shells slipped to the wayside as several women opened to being seen in their deepest heartache and challenge.

In honor and testament to each woman's courageous 'dark night of the soul', I offer only my personal sharing below from this time. May this forever bless the great transition we each pass through to find the incomprehensible place within that remains in trust and service against all odds...

There is a point I have reached where I just cannot turn back from. My body feels bruised and battered, twisted and cranked out of alignment. Whether I have done this or another, no longer matters. Whether it was because I am human, distorted or sacred no longer holds distinction. Where I am at simply does not feel right. Yet here I am and none of this can be wrong. What have I given my life for? I can no longer tell or see... I can no longer feel or even care. My greatest prayer is for you – beloved – to fill all the pages of my life with your utmost wisdom. I hurt beyond knowing how much I can hurt. The emptiness of my spirit wishes only for you to fill me up. Where to turn when I no longer want anything from this world? Where to go when all I envisioned no longer feeds my deeper longing. Dearest God I long for you in a way I can no longer express or give form to. I long to be by your side in a way that feels like complete death. Should it feel otherwise??... You smile upon me and share, Let it feel as it does. Nothing otherwise will satisfy you. The death you long for is your ultimate salvation. Let it come and completely wash all else away. Sweet daughter, holy wife, let my arms encurl you forever in your glory. I wish to tell you a thousand times over that you are the majesty of my world. Will you take that in – will you sit there in my embrace and allow me to completely adore you? My love for you cannot be forgotten or cast aside. It does not matter what another does to you... it will never compare to how much I love and cherish you. You are my beloved wife – my glory – the heart of my world. Can you feel that? Drink me in through every portal and pore of your being. I will saturate you in a dream beyond understanding. I will saturate you in a fountain of sheer homecoming. Care not about this outside landscape. Feel my love for all of creation – steady, steadily. And feel my love for you at the core. I wish for you to know this beyond anything else. Beyond the flow of your next breath. I cherish you so deeply. My will for you is to be at One with me, with Her, with it all... Love, your Divine Masculine nature

~ *FACES OF THE MOTHER*, SECOND TOUCHSTONE EXPRESSION

ↈ

Mutual Care & Crafting

Throughout our journey I offered each Life Artist an opportunity for two personal phone check-ins. This served our deepening resonance and provided support and healing for the overall creative process. This also helped us navigate and tend practical details along the way.

Our time on the phone was intimate and revealing. I got to sense and feel the depth these women were working from throughout this process. It was a tender experience to connect in this way. I learned about mutual care – how each woman was tending the dreams of my heart as I was supporting her in her own. These women had become my comrades and co-journeyers. I was a sister and guide. I was witnessing and directly participating in *Faces of the Mother* being born through us all.

Knowing many of the women beforehand through various contexts of my work and personal life, these phone connections allowed us to feel who we had been to each other and what we were now becoming. We got to reorient to where we were in time and space. With those I hadn't met before, these connections were opportunities to sense each other's core essence and feel into what had drawn us together. We discussed the spectrum of each woman's creations and process, how things were taking shape, and about the journey and internal experience. I offered an intuitively crafted meditation/process if it arose, blessing each woman upon her path. Each Artist's process was a gift to me. Her wisdom became an opportunity for our feminine creativity and expression to soar free.

The testament that what we give to others returns to us manifold was alive and validated here. *Faces of the Mother* formed because I wanted to discover something for myself and give something into the fabric of the feminine. I wanted to celebrate authentic expression through women and mothers, and for all future generations. I'd been willing to face whatever would come in this process. We cannot know the path of our journey, but we can choose to face it in our wholeness and softened resolution. Rooting in to our mutual care and crafting, we will create no matter what. Through our hands and hearts, we can choose how these creations will be expressed and exposed.

One early Saturday morning I was sitting at the farthest reaches of my yard ready to connect with one of the woman. It was our first round of calls, about four weeks into our process. It was mid-August and no one else in my home was stirring. The chickens and ducks made soft sounds in the background as the morning light bathed the yard. I sat beside our garden, noticing in such a short time intense growth had occurred.

I felt a weight in my heart. Our family had been searching for our cat, Onyx, all week. He hadn't come home one evening, which was uncharacteristic of his nature. I now sat in this inexplicable place where joy and grief collide. I breathed, opening my heart to this Life Artist I'd never met. I said a prayer, honoring my garden, this process, the woman and Mother I would be talking to, and touched my longing to be reunited with our cat.

Immediately on the phone this woman's mystical charm and gifts touched me. She shared her artistic vision, to create thirteen gifts through her inner seeing for each of the *Faces of the Mother* Artists as a way to honor our interconnected work. She carried the intentions for this project so deeply, without me having said anything. It touched my heart. I felt co-creation awakening and was reminded how we were in this together on every level.

As this Artist and I talked she asked, "Is that your cat meowing in the background?" Though none of my cats were around, I opened up and shared how ours was missing. She described the cat she sensed, and saw him as being black. Onyx was black. Tears filled my eyes. In showing up for another in the fullness of myself, the most unexpected gifts were received. That morning a healing space was created to rest in my deepest heartache, joy *and* longing, not having to choose one over the other. This Life Artist was by my side, aiding me through this restorative gift of mutual care and feminine crafting.

Cauldron of Initiation

To enter the landscape of our inherent creativity, we go through our own initiation and way of being with it. I have come to know this as simply how we choose to "live our lives" in each moment.

In our modern culture and spiritual circles, we've portrayed great initiations as coming from someone or something outside of us... a teacher, spiritual tradition, a healing or life experience. Yet what often falls beneath the radar in lieu of upholding this externalization of power, is the reality that initiation happens on the inner realm and occurs *because* a shift has been made within. This awakens not through the self as a separate being, but arising out of one's personal deepening into the collective experience of life and the nature of our interrelational reality.

This brings true initiation into focus as the old adage proclaims, "When the student is ready, the teacher appears," acknowledging transformation and living within a new reality occurs through 'calling in'. This is what science has discovered with the fertilization of an egg within a woman. The egg calls in the sperm, drawing it into the uterus. A woman invites, welcomes and *permits* the entrance of creation at the most fundamental and self-centering level. This is a valuing of our feminine legacy, and is vastly different than the prior notions we've held that the sperm pushes its way into an egg. Here there is a mutual synergy of push/pull, invite/accept/welcome, initiation and invitation, allowing and opening. A Feminine Life Artist calls in life... inviting, allowing and absorbing the deeper alchemical components for her inner transformation and initiation to occur.

By its very nature the feminine is the receptive portal that is the hallmark of initiation coming into action. Through the process of surrender, letting go into the deeper realms of one's own being, you become the magnetic force that draws all that will help to adjust, reorient and bring to life the truths of yourself and sacred reality. The feminine nature of our being welcomes the fullness of change into her soul, heart and body, inviting it to do as it will to help her grow, heal, transform and become more of who she is designed to be. And this is not through outside or separate measures, but through the deepest wellspring of our unification in connection to all aspects of life.

Through our *Faces of the Mother* journey, each Life Artist entered her own pathway of initiation through the unique makeup of her experience. The ways this revealed were as unique as each woman, yet the deepening initiations were similar in their themes, frequency and resulting realizations. The timing and rhythm of such catalyzing events coincided with similar patterns within each of the women's lives. Life Artists would comment, "It's like she's sharing a piece of my own experience." "Through her words I see myself and what I'm really feeling."

To initiate means to 'begin, start or commence... to enroll, incorporate, induct, install." In spiritual tradition, initiation is the cornerstone of entering a particular path for learning a tradition, often benchmarked through ritual and ceremony. What occurs for the initiate is seen in light of what one must prepare for, go through and face to be ready to receive the new teachings and wisdom.

Within the context of the *Faces of the Mother* journey, initiation occurred *because* each woman said Yes! to her life, wisdom and natural creativity coming forth. An initiation occurred because she had *already* prepared. Life Artists were ready to engage with the changes of their lives, whether or not they knew what was coming or the details of the form these changes would take.

This is what occurs for a woman during pregnancy and birth. A mother is ready to bring her baby into the world because she and her baby, in mutual body and soul, are ready to move into this next stage of expression and distinction. Our minds, intellect or emotions may not always feel such readiness, but our bodies, souls, relationships and life's reflections know the truth. The more we trust this allowance, the more all aspects of us begin to work in congruency, just like a babe being born.

The experiences of our outer world are the result of our inner proclamation of Yes! to our own lives as they are. As Feminine Life Artists learned to let their resounding Yes! to being a vessel of sacred expression be their foundation, the transformation within their lives and reality was confirmation that this inner resilience to the nature of themselves was being born.

Into the Deep

To deeply enter this domain of initiation, I offer snapshots below from our Life Artists sharing what they were originally drawn to with this project, and what *actually* happened within them along the way. Through their own words we get the clearest glimpse into the intensity, unknowingness, blessings and surprises that occurred through the terrain of our self-source-creative initiation. This is a celebration of our life and how creation is naturally born and breathes through our unique being.

Through this resounding willingness to long to be all that we can be, we are drawn into the experiences that remake us from the inside out, aiding us in becoming more of who we are.

The questions I presented to each Life Artist were:

- What is it you hoped to accomplish by responding to the *Faces of the Mother* invitation?

- How did you envision this work and process would impact your life? Has it? Have you allowed it?

- What has occurred thus far for you personally, creatively and soulfully in your relationship to yourself and your artistic expression?

- How have you changed? How have you become more of who you are? What has fallen away?

- What matters most to you now?

℞

Here are the Artists' stories and expressions. Here is the face and wisdom of Sacred Initiation...

I wanted to challenge myself to be part of a collaboration, and to work on a subject that I've only addressed in a very abstract way. I was curious about the project because it came into my life so suddenly, the deadline being the day I received the invitation! I don't usually jump into creative work, but I was compelled to just do it.

I imagined it would be something I worked on in a more scheduled way than I usually work on projects. It started out scheduled, and my life pretty immediately went sideways, taking the schedule with it. I didn't want to allow that wildness, but I ended up, in several instances, having no choice. I imagined it would be part of the natural flow of things I was already working on. In some ways that turned out to be true, but it also opened up new ways of working, i.e.: fitting creative time into crazy circumstances, and seemingly less than ideal workspaces.

I have become very aware of barriers, roadblocks and pretty much the great wall of china, constructed between my everyday idea/experience of 'mother' and my secret idea of 'mothering.' I've never confronted the conflict directly in art, it's always been hidden under other themes. I've really become clear about moving the thinking brain out of the art process, unless I need to use a ruler. I've learned I can find space to make things in just about any situation, emotional or physical. It's been great to realize that I don't need dedicated studio space, let alone a dedicated table, to get in the right frame of mind for making art.

My long-term relationship has fallen away, my physical body has gone through hell and back, and my emotional state has been rather treacherous to navigate. I have been able to get to the simple essence of what's important, and how to put one foot in front of the other. again. What has fallen away and returned? belief, compassion, clarity. I've gotten more aware of my need to have a creative project in my life, no matter what's going on around it. I feel happier when I have something in the works, even if things are going haywire in my day-to-day life.

What matters most to me now? Letting myself find ways to make things, even if there's no deadline or goal in sight. A pot of soup, a peaceful hour, expressing myself creatively, remembering that 'there but by the grace of god go I' when interacting with others, and the knowledge that these few things are really, truly full of treasures. ~ Lori

൪

I felt a deep calling to participate in this project, but I also couldn't fathom how I would add one more thing to my already busy life. I also couldn't wrap my head around exactly what I would be creating and what the 'commitment' to this project really looked like, but I could think of all the ways it just wouldn't work... and so I let the first call for artists pass me by. With that I felt a DEEP sadness that I had not followed that guidance inside of myself. Damn, why had I let that pass me by... and then the second sweep was offered and even though I was so saddened that I had let the first opportunity pass me by, the fear crept back in and I almost let the opportunity slip by yet again...

And now I'm here, in this place that is perfect for me. I feel a connectedness to myself that I have never experienced. This journey has led me to the light inside myself that I always knew was there...

This project has reminded me to TRUST myself... to KNOW myself... to CHERISH myself... to LOVE myself... to HEAL myself... I want to stay connected to this feeling always. It is the light that helps guide me on this journey to the deep dark cavernous places of my heart and soul. I want to know these places and embrace them... always. ~ Krisiey

 G

I didn't know what would come. I was delighted and honored to receive the invitation – it felt very life affirming to be seen as an artist and connected to Spirit. Ultimately, I was hoping to get into deeper connection with the "feminine" aspect of God.

I couldn't have any idea for how it would go. The only expectation I had was in the logistical sense: I would have a guide for the artistic process & deadlines (so helpful!). To say this process has impacted my life would be a gross understatement. This process became my life, or my life became the process. I have allowed it mostly, and also resisted and then suffered. I am learning to nurture what I'm experiencing as 'difficult' – just love and care for myself as I would a sad child. I'm also learning to just get the fuck up like an adult! Just keep walking, right into it, right through it. Sad is how I feel? Yep, sad. Scared is how I feel? Yep, scared. Just keep walking. One foot in front of the other.

I have evolved a really deep understanding for mental health. Most of this comes from the effect "stuff" has – too much, the environmental impact, the feeling in a space filled/unoccupied with stuff. This has become really clear. I'm also really connecting to the sensitivities I have always had to fall so deeply in love with people, objects, places – it is profound and "new" to experience this in such a sudden and deep way. I touch people more – physically – I just put my hand on a shoulder or arm when we're talking. So much of my life I have been so concerned about making other people feel comfortable (is it okay for this person to have me reach out right now, for instance) – and that can be so confusing! It adds such a confused energy to interactions. I've learned that what makes anyone feel really comfortable is being with someone who is comfortable with themself. That courage gives everyone the freedom to be exactly who we are – and it's a freedom not a demand.

What is falling away is the pleasing. I just have better boundaries now. It's still not totally comfortable as a habit, but it's clearer and more respectful of myself.

What matters most? Hmmm. I want to say love because I want that to matter most but the first answer is actually: integrity. It's a crystal clean form of love. There, I have both! And I love when other people have integrity but I spend more time now attuning to myself (have I kept my word? am I clear? does that have integrity? do I need to apologize?). So, my own integrity is more important to me. Instead of being bogged down by what is going badly "over there", I am focusing on what I can do "right here." ~ Sarah

ᘒ

I hoped to reawaken the artist within and connect with other strong women.

I envisioned an adventure. Connecting with my innermost self. The adventure was darker than I anticipated, and I found myself resisting the 'work'. I think I was afraid of going deep, and once I did I found a lack of love for myself. It affected me profoundly.

I did reawaken the artist within, and that has been very healing for me. I've made life-altering decisions that allow me to honor myself, which was lacking before. Art is so healing, and in reconnecting with my art I have rediscovered new pathways to the soul. Unspeakable bonds to my innermost being.

I've made a decision to release the fear. That's huge for me. And my life is changing drastically, with a future more uncertain than ever before. But I've learned to trust myself, and in doing so have realized that I AM the strong woman I want to be.

Everything is connected. I used to feel a disconnect, and that showed in my relationships to others and in the way I lived my life. I've found that in honoring myself, I honor everyone and everything. Right now, I find it most important to honor myself first. (although it still feels really weird and selfish to say that). ~ Holly

ℭ℟

I wanted to be remembered. To join with others in the artistic process, even on a weird spiritual level... and it worked! To challenge myself to come up with and finish a work of art; to join a journey which has woven me into an indescribable weave with 12 other women. I think I envisioned myself finding myself completely... hearing the voice which would tell me which way to go in my life. I am 40 and finding a new pathway of career... and love.

I was awakening already, and realizing that with life going on (and all the pulling of me), I needed to MAKE time to do my art. I have allowed it. I had to dedicate time for it, and for me – for the creative life inside of me. No longer can I wait for inspiration. I must seek it out.

My eyes are opened. I am truly a jewel – seeing more and more of my gorgeous and naturally occurring facets every day. Oh, hello! There's another one! Stunning!! I certainly feel more connected. I want to always be involved in a project like this to connect me back into my creative spirit and dedicate myself to allowing The Goddess to move through me.

What has fallen away? The need for perfection...the desire to please others above myself... the requirement to clean my house before I begin working on my art. Friends have fallen away. I feel much more free now to be myself and to spend more time doing the things I love: writing, singing, dancing, playing with my children....

What matters most to me now? My soul and play. And love? It always has. But now it's more focused. As I have entered the "Mother" part of my journey, I no longer have the urges I used to – such as parachuting, bungee jumping or rock-climbing. Now it is enough (and then some) for me to give my time to my family and send love into the world in different ways. Not so much ego now, more giving. ~ Anna

ℭ℟

When I received the invitation, a call to be a Life Artist, it was a moment of synchronicity. I wanted to re-engage with creativity in my life and I was also intrigued by this notion of Mother as Leader. It was an opportunity to explore leadership using the creative arts. I envisioned several playful hours reconnecting with creative tools: coloured pencils, watercolours, drawing, painting, collaging images, and more. I quickly discovered it wasn't the 'creative arts' that was the focus. It was the 'creative process' that became the stage itself! The action and activity was to become aware, reflective, and present to the creative process unfolding.

Mother as Leader led and supported me in a process of reflecting, transforming and living deeper questions:

How do I create my life experience?

How can I live in alignment: body, mind, spirit & with divine mystery?

What does it mean to open up to expressing the fullest potential, the divine nature of my own being, of my Soul?

Creativity arises each moment. Creativity is an expression of Life. I can be artistic with the use of art supplies. Yet it also occurs in ordinary day to day activities. It is my choice of words, the direction of thinking, the range of my feelings, the movement of my body, the flow of my breathing.

I discovered the Face of Mother as Leader, for me, means to be led towards connecting inward and creatively expressing outward what is occurring in my life. I am deepening in my ability to listen. Through creativity I can share what I understand, know, see, sense and feel. By engaging in creative expression, I can pause, trust and express my truth.

What matters most to me now? To continue engaging and learning in this creative process called Life! ~ Catherine G.

CR

By accepting the invitation to participate in the 'Faces of the Mother' project, I hoped to maintain an open heart and mind in order to see in which direction the voice would lead me. I wanted to remain open, like a blank slate, without any preconceived notion or expectation.

I set for myself the question of what it would be like to understand and translate the distinct vision of another person (Sharon Ann Rose of Faces of the Mother) and try to truly hear that voice and meld it, harmonize it, to my own and see how the outcome would play out. I have to say, it has been a bumpy ride; feelings of doubt and fear crept in from time to time. However, with the transmissions, with time and allowing for whatever it was to show up, I did allow the process to move me. It has been an interesting time. I envisioned this process to be very dynamic because it was not something I had ever done before. I was having a dialogue not only with myself but with someone I had not yet met. I would say that it did impact my life in very positive ways, even through the trials of uncertainty and clouded vision. In the end, by allowing both the dialogue and the silence, I felt like the voice was heard and manifested.

For me, it feels like every single time before a canvas or a stone or what have you, it feels like the first time. I had thought, perhaps, that it somehow gets easier but I find that I am always on the edge of not knowing and maybe, for now, I have to accept that and just move from that space. This was similar, and yet different, because, again, I was in the not knowing, but now, it was with someone else with her own distinct vision. I think the dialogue was provocative as it was discourse with another person, not the stone trying to tell me its form but this person. From there, I could hear those words and see how my heart and hands worked and created. This challenge and process, ultimately, reinforced me as an artist. I plumbed the depths and came back up again.

I think that the challenge of trusting oneself to hear and listen to another, then to turn and hear and listen to oneself is first and foremost a relational act: something has been exchanged. It is from here that an idea is shaped and kneaded, and it's through this dialogue, in all its facets, that a form begins to take shape, and hopefully, is born. I hope that I have become more of who I am. As for something falling away, if, when I turn in my expression, I find myself satisfied with the piece, truly sated by it, and without worry about other people's reactions or approval, then that piece of doubt will fall away. I do feel I have grown from it. Every time one has to confront something within themself and commit to staying with it, despite the falls and doubts, then there is growth. Growth and the acceptance of the gift that surfaced.

What matters most is staying true to my reading of something. I really want to trust myself and the voice(s) that is within me. I do not want to look outside for validation. What matters most is the belief that my voice, my truth, is good enough and worthy just because it is. ~ Catherine D.

☙

I had long wanted to bring this wild eyed priestess to life. This seemed the perfect opportunity.

Every work requires process. This particular work required a different level of commitment because she was very far inside of me...a part of my ancestors. I had to search for her and draw her out.

I've had the notion in my head of change being associated with difficulty. The past several seasons have made me realize that is not necessarily true. Every idea or situation is birthed in one way or another. Easy or hard, painful or not. I'm learning to let it happen and embrace the scenario. I've let go of what I can't control. It's futile to attempt to force anything on this level of existence. I'm letting the universe flow around me and observing the changes in my consciousness.

What matters most to me now? Really, the same things that have always mattered to me... I love my family, friends, nature and this amazing journey that I set out on many years ago. ~ Dana

☙

I wasn't sure what this is or would be, even the end goal was a mystery at first. In some ways, it still is. It helped me overcome resistance and really want to contribute and be part of something new. I stepped out and began to listen more deeply and step by step; it continues to be revealed...

Again, I didn't know how this would impact my life. It is good having a reason and some reasonable accountability to accomplish something artistically. This is so much more and so much happier than just that, however. I am learning to accept my own process in a new and deeper place, like moving on to a different plane and experiencing deeper truth. Still so much to do and learn. Learn and do. Still, just be. Much happens there. I AM. I am allowing ~ in ways I do not even understand yet. I do feel lasting change inside.

It has all become okay. There is much grace. More than I knew and more than I allowed. Whatever I come up with, wherever I am at, it is ALL okay. It is significant in my growth to thoroughly desire joining in.

I am deeply in process. I am becoming. I am a paradox. I am at peace.

What matters most to me now? Continuing on. Having a louder voice. Truly enjoying what is. Contributing what is uniquely mine! ~ Connie

CR

PART TWO
A COLLABORATION

∞

A Bit About Archetypes ~ the backbone of our journey

Our *Faces of the Mother* journey engaged and passed through the archetypal expressions of the Sacred Feminine. In this section, you will be introduced and become intimate with these living archetypes within.

The word *archetype* comes from the Latin noun, *archetypum*, which translates as "first-molded". Archetypes are a principle pattern from which others are copied.[1] They provide a template for discovering the mythic and symbolic nature of our world and selves.

As we engage with sacred archetypes, we discover aspects of ourselves and culture that are larger than we can often comprehend, and thus these parts may have gone unnoticed, hidden, been repressed or played down in some way throughout our lifetime and over centuries. As we journey through our lives, exploring our cultural conditioning and evolutionary passage, we call upon these archetypal expressions in an effort to reclaim something within ourselves, and to learn about the holistic and multi-layered aspect of our reality.

The archetypes used in *Faces of the Mother* were inspired from the original 13 Sacred Feminine archetypes that are the cornerstone of Ariel Spilsbury's teachings and work.[2] Ariel is a "mumbling mystic" and "planetary midwife" who has been serving and honoring the feminine through her writings, mentorship and Mystery School.

A journey through the Archetypal Faces of the Divine Feminine
is an inner roadmap, an entryway into the Mystery offering a
holographic form and alchemical map for your consciousness to
effortlessly enter into a higher order of reality with ecstasy and joy.
~ ARIEL SPILSBURY, FROM *THE 13 MOON ORACLE*[3]

---

1   Wikipedia, the free encyclopedia - http://en.wikipedia.org

2   Ariel Spilsbury - http://holographicgoddess.com/

3   13 Feminine Archetypes & Oracles – http://holographicgoddess.com/products/oracles

After engaging with these 13 archetypes brought forth through Ariel, I was drawn to go deeper into the first and original one... into the Great Mother. I sensed this would have an impact and significance, not only for my journey, but also for the path of others. By focusing on, opening to and going ever-deeper into the wonders of the Mother, my intention was to explore and grow intimate with Her many forms and expressions, and unearth something within myself rooted in my modern-day and ancestral journey as woman and mother. I imagined this would impact the way I'd related to creation, and with the way I perceived creation worked. I longed to touch and connect in a new way with the original wounds I carried in relationship to life, love, my own mother and sense of self. The 13 archetypes I used here are rooted in the wisdom of the original one – in the primordial and primary Mother.

The *Faces of the Mother* archetypes are not meant to replace or in any way remake the original 13 archetypes of the Sacred Feminine. They are a doorway into the unlimited nature of every aspect of life, and what can occur as we plunge in, allowing ourselves to validate the wisdom growing from within. This self-creative and initiatory process helps us turn another key, open another handle, to peer unabashedly and non-judgmentally at ourselves as we breathe, wonder and simply ask, "So what else exists within me and this life?"

Please refer to the alchemical work of Ariel Spilsbury [1] for an understanding of the original 13 Sacred Feminine archetypes.

To enact this archetypal pathway through the intimate journey you are about to begin, I bow to and honor all that has come before, laying this foundation for all to come through this precious interconnected life.

Prayer

Kneeling at my bedside as a child, I learned the art and intimacy of prayer. Through a path of faith, longing and confusion, and the grief stricken moments of my human development and growth, I felt its scorch of passion. From the soul

---

1   Ariel Spilsbury's work - http://holographicgoddess.com/

of a woman who's been a mother, lover, leader, healer, sister, daughter, writer and human being, I've known the process of annihilation that holds you in the flames until all that is left is ashes. It can be hard to retain our innocence, commitment and faith in the divine nature of reality through whatever is to come.

Through prayer we discover our vulnerability. We allow ourselves to no longer be in control, to think we have it all figured out, to believe we can 'go it alone.' No matter who or what we are praying to, through prayer we have the potential to surrender all we thought we were and were becoming, to engage our purpose, guidance and restoration for who we are drawn to be. This is the field of our inner creative fire, where we no longer judge ourselves in its intensity.

To release and face our personal and collective notions about what prayer is and should be, is to forge one's own sacred expression and pathway through these almighty waters. This is a sincere path for embodying our holiness and humility, glimpsing our divinity and humanity. Our prayers are *our* way of living and breathing, loving and hurting. They are the heartache we leave at the door each time we walk away, and the tears that flow unbridled each time we are embraced upon our return. Our prayers are the place we drop into when nothing of this world can soothe our human aches or provide a sense of direction. To pray is to open our hands to life. They are done with our heart, arms and eyes wide open to what stands before and within us.

Engaging with creation is to listen to the truth within oneself, and speaking it in earnest before our sense of source, our beginning and end. It is a mutual exchange of listening, loving and learning, taking in, pausing, distilling, letting go to hear what only we can hear in the ways we do, and tending to and cherishing this like we would a newborn babe. Our prayers are a place where our sense of spirit and matter meld, growing into the fires of our yet-formed manifest expression of thoughts, longings, words, cries and deeds. Our prayers bring fantasies alive so we can be honest about where we are injuring and denying our innocence, and where we have grown deaf to our wisdom and maturity. Through our willingness to get on our knees and stand emboldened before life, we proclaim we are in relationship to love's force. Through these cries and proclamations, through our intentions and inspirations, we come to know what we believe and will face on behalf of our world through whatever will come.

When our hearts align with our souls, when our wombs align with our minds, when our feminine and masculine nature comes together, life is born, living on through the breath of creation.

Our voyage through these Mother Faces grew out of this longing to become who we are. Prayer was offered as my way of connecting with creation. It is how I intimately talk with and receive love's wisdom by no other name.

May we allow our lives to become the living prayers they long to become.

Here is the prayer of our *Faces of the Mother* initiation. Into creative self-initiation, plunging into this journey with all that we are...

dearest Life, dearest Love
my beloved Mother
in abiding connection with my Divine Father
I ask that you carry me now into the womb of my heart and soul
Into the original place where I was created from
so I might experience a tangible remembrance of all that I am and can be.
Support me beloved life
in reclaiming the dignity of my sacred creation.
Help all parts of my being heal, restore and restructure
around the true essence of my self.
Hold me close upon this journey
hold me closer when I forget and stray from who I am and who you know me to be.
Hold me closer still when I deny, denigrate and discredit the value of my heart
and my creative endeavors.
May all that comes through me bless all forever.
I celebrate my heart carried in love's sacred hands, always.

~ *FACES OF THE MOTHER*, INITIATING PRAYER

☙

Mother Faces

It began with a prayer... to know the fullest scope of the Sacred Feminine within my own being. It moved into a shared journey, walking beside others in collaborative discovery.

The Mother comes alive through our fullest living and the vast authenticity we each share. This provides collaboration – of women, life and creativity – through our personal work and shared reflection. We learn we are in this together, crafting life by how we translate each experience and what we choose to do within this intimacy we hold with the divine.

Into the full scope of our Mother Faces these Feminine Life Artists were beckoned, growing intimate with 13 archetypal expressions I'd greeted and refined through my own motherhood passage. This vital weave was offered into the warp threads of our journey to establish a living intimacy with our creative center.

Holding this foundation as a gift to be shared, my heart's call was an invitation welcoming sisters, friends, colleagues, co-journeyers and creators on an inner voyage... a passage through the landscape of the Mother within. Through the terrain of the Mother as Mystic, Artist and Healer, as Distiller, Decomposer and Midwife, as Leader, Regenerator and Priestess, as Bestower, Beloved and Unifier, our tribe traveled.

Each woman was connected to 1 Mother Face, and two artists engaged with 2. I committed to walk beside them through it all. Each week I engaged with one Mother Face and her partnering Artist through a natural progression and rhythm. We set off on what we could not know as each woman dove into personal intimacy with her creative fertility to see what would reveal.

Many wondered how each Artist was connected to her particular Face. The accuracy each woman felt, what unfolded through her life experience, and the inherent wisdom that awakened, was startling. It revealed how the natural workings and wonder of life unfold.

In my original invitation I asked participants to share which Mother Face(s) they were drawn to. Some shared a few, others many, one left it open, and one artist wished for one specific face. Anchoring in to my original intention to support women through their direct intimacy with the Mother, I gathered these dream seeds and made sacred offerings to each woman's hopes, wisdom and longing. I prayed, asking whichever Mother Face would best serve each Artist to reveal. Through a fluid process of connecting each woman to her Face and offering up the 2 extras to those who expressed prior interest for more than 1, everyone was matched with an archetypal correspondent to walk with through this journey.

Nothing was shared from the onset of the Mother Faces except their name. Out of respect for the workings of our inherent soul fertility and creativity, I wanted to support each woman in birthing her life through this intimate and personal partnership. We set off to find our deepest self-valuing, trusting we each would hear, see, feel and intuit through our own bodies, hearts, voices and minds.

One of the resolute gifts of the *Faces of the Mother* process was that nothing was predetermined, dictated or placed on top of our adventure to create external boundaries for a woman's creative process. The landscape arose from what lived within, uniquely and collectively, and how we were attuning to that. I chose to hold the Mother Faces in the vast mystery as we set off together, beginning where we were, on common ground.

This is the gift the Mother holds for us. And this is the gift we can choose to receive within ourselves, circulating it through our history so we might fully enter the present, sharing our presence with all. We've been indoctrinated by a historical lineage and social construct that tells us from the outside what something is, how it should feel, what it should look like, and its greatest value and purpose. Learning to reclaim our inner Mother heritage can be a daunting passage as we reorient to endless voices that have grown too-accustomed inside our minds and psyches, telling us what life is and is meant to be.

Unlike a "free form" arena, our *Faces of the Mother* process had very clear parameters and boundaries, a solid sense of connection and rooting, and a rhythm we recommitted to no matter where the internal voices tried to take us. This is an important and pivotal distinction to be made. Throughout my work with women and mothers, I've seen how the feminine can get lost in fluidity and formlessness, and in 'the other'. She moves with the tides of life and change, and thus can forget the masculine gifts of showing up for herself and what wishes to be created and expressed through her distinction. The qualities of steadfastness, structure and self-focus are often worked with through our masculine nature. As we come into intimacy with the Mother we learn to trust our innocence and no longer judge ourselves and the natural balance of our inherent Masculine and Feminine energy. It is here we accept who we are as we are, and show up to life in our simplified being.

There is a resonant balance that grows and prospers inside each of us as we tend our Feminine and Masculine natures. This is unique to, yet congruent with all of life. This balance is struck as we fully engage with our feminine receptivity, letting constraints and constrictions fall away, while deeply healing and revering our relationship with our masculine sovereignty and protection, allowing the full force of our commitment to love and self guide us.

Engaging with the Mother Faces through an internally focused barometer, aided these Life Artists to let go of what they perceived about themselves, life, art and the workings of creation. They explored their own value, worth, sense of purpose and possibility by learning to validate themselves. And through an externally focused measure of rhythm and mutual connection, these women returned to our prior established commitments, receiving accountable touchstones and remembering why we said Yes! to this process in the first place. This provided a framework to see and draw upon the vast array of support that was available, even in our darkest hour.

During our 3-month journey each Feminine Life Artist listened to, grappled and played with, contemplated, was inspired by and torn to pieces from these Mother Faces. She learned to trust and heal through her direct connection with her soul fertility and creative process. Intimizing with each Face and letting that guide women into expression and form through their own hands, voice, writing and life, brought unexpected discoveries, deep healing, heart wrenching change and life appreciation.

We share with you now what was crafted through this journey, knowing that through us and each aspect of life, the vastness of the Mother is found.

I pray to you, for I know She dwells within your soul.
I pray for you, for I know She is born through your being.
I pray with you, for I know you are my reflection.
I pray, for I know we are Her daughters
falling in love with ourselves within Her grace.

ℭℜ

As you peruse these words, artwork, reflections and images, may you be drawn deeper within to the place untouched by this world. It is available and ready to guide you in creating the beauty you see, remember, taste, touch and will intimately come to know. May these creative works ignite your longing to be in direct relationship with the wisdom of the Mother, and may you surrender to Her expression so we may all find who we are and can be.

Presentation

The Mother Faces of our collection are presented through a rhythmic and intimate format.

Through each of our 13 Faces you will find a...

PASSAGE: this section shares the felt experience of each Mother Face. This is the wisdom I encountered as I held this archetype close, praying with and for the particular artist working with Her, and journeying with my surrender into Her voice and guidance.

BLESSING: this section shares the energetic blessing of each Mother Face. This is what I felt well up within as I held this archetype close, praying with and for the particular artist working with this Mother Face, and surrendering to Her voice and guidance. These blessings are shared in the direct voice of each Mother Face.

PRAYER: this section shares my personal longing to embody each of the Mother Faces. This is what I felt arise through my wish to access and embody this quality of the Mother. It is offered through a prayer to all of creation.

WISDOM: this section shares the deeper contemplations into this quality of the Mother Face. This is what I learned as I engaged with and wondered about each archetype, and its deeper implications for all of humanity.

ENGAGEMENT: this section offers creative suggestions to engage with the energies of each Mother Face and journey into your own intimacy with Her. No matter what you choose to do or not do here, She will be with you, aiding you in birthing your full expression into the world.

ARTIST INSIGHT & OFFERINGS: this section provides quotes, snippets, photos and images from each of the artist's journeys into the depths of her Mother Face and creative process. It vulnerably portrays what these women discovered and how working with these qualities transformed them.

IN HER INTIMACY – INITIATIONS & GIFTS: this section offers a simplified pathway of initiation and an integrated gift from each Mother Face. This is the true celebration of Her, providing a connection between what came through me during our *Faces of the Mother* journey and through each artist. This section is a doorway into the personal pilgrimage you are ready for if you choose to take this intimate walk with the Faces of the Mother in your own life.

DREAMING: in the empty white spaces at the end of each Mother Face section, please dream with and as each archetype... breathing Her alive through you. Doodle. Draw. Jot down your own wisdom from this intimate connection to the multi-faceted nature of your Feminine Soul.

❧ Mother as Mystic

© LORI WOOLF

The Mystic lives from her womb,
and the deeper ocean of her being.

Passage

She carries you to the ocean of your being, where you may know yourself beyond time, name or role you've played in this life. She offers you the gift of seeing what is often not seen, hearing what often goes unheard, and feeling what is often not picked up on or brushed aside in our fast-paced culture. She invites you to imagine your inner world like a day at the beach, where you lie upon the sand napping below the sun, allowing the warmth above and below to envelop you, as you are cradled in the natural restoration of your deepest surrender. These mystical qualities awakened in oneself allow a deeper insight to come forth in time of strife or of ease. It is the capacity to move from the essence of your being, reclaiming the pearls of wisdom that only a deep-seated comfort in your own nature will bring.

Blessing

I am the part of you wise beyond your years, yet forever like a child. I come to you in moments of sacred play, through the games of our hearts and the times when we are willing to wonder and to let go. I form expression from deep inside your womb, like a seed growing under the warm, nurturing care of the sun shining upon the ocean waters. You will find me here, nestled in the folds of your core – always still, always watching, listening. When you call upon me I rise like the moon to be born through you, bringing light and deeper awareness even into your darkest hour. Each prayer of your soul is heard by me. Believe in my love to guide you through each rise and fall of your own tides. ~ *Mother as Mystic*

Prayer

Dearest Life ~ Dearest Love

Draw me into the oceans of myself, so I may touch and experience the mystical qualities of my being. Help me look at, heal and reaffirm these deeper truths of my nature. Support me to go beyond my own understanding of what is possible, to resurrect my own Face as the Mystic. May I cleanse all past beliefs, hurts and wounding I've placed on myself and others in connecting to the true capabilities, capacities and gifts of the Mystic within. This journey I cannot make alone. Sacred Mother, help me restore my deeper whole nature in your name. Help me feel the presence of my sisters and my brothers, and all of life beside me, returning us to our innocence and true power. May this bless my life and all those lives I touch forevermore. Amen.

Wisdom

It is so important in our current culture to reclaim this inherent quality of the Mystic. The Sacred Feminine is restored each time a woman believes in herself and in her knowing. Once upon a time it was the women who were turned to, to reveal the workings and mysteries of life. It was known and felt how intuitively connected to the earth's rhythms and cycles they were. In many indigenous cultures, the dreams of menstruating women were relied upon to reveal greater insight for the community at large. In many societies people inherently knew that when a woman is pregnant (with child, project or vision), she is more attuned to the spiritual realms.

These qualities of the mystic within a woman, within a mother, within us all, are what authentically guide our culture, families, relationships and selves. This is the wisdom of the ages awakening through us so we might express a deeper truth within each circumstance and moment.

It is through remembering the worth of oneself as a mystical artist that the sacred cycles of life and our hearts are restored.

The Mystic is that which knows beyond our knowing, and then
carries the pearl of this through us to be made known in form.

Engagement with the Mystic

- Go for a walk at the ocean.

- Listen to the tides, waves and moon.

- Play with children and animals.

- Ask your inner knowing what it would do in each circumstance.

- Share your deeper truth with those you trust.

- Remain silent, watchful and listening.

- Feel what the plants and trees are offering, respond to them.

- Create an artistic piece to express yourself as the Mystic.

- Say this within your heart, "I am a Mother. I am a Mystic."

- Nurture the qualities of innocence, wonder and trust within.

- Create and then let go of the outcome/expression. See what lives ever deeper inside your creations.

- Keep a dream journal, jotting down visions from your day and evening dreams.

- When menstruating, honor your blood and the energies moving through you. Offer your blood to the earth in ritual. Offer your visions to your heart in prayer.

Artist Insight & Offerings

...what if we have each and all experienced the complete, atomic love of the mother, and we are each and all longing to feel it again, even for a split second? and, we are all questioning whether we're imagining the memory of something that happened before we got here, and happens beyond the 3-dimensions. what if so much suffering is the feeling of the loss and longing, with no-one to tell us it's not our imagination?

~ Lori, our Mystic

This painting started as a discernable face, then shifted to geometric patterns, changing once again to small portraits, and finally settling on a split second of abstracted feeling. Layers upon layers.

I wanted the portrait to look like 'something.' I was hoping it would morph back to one of the more recognizable stages. Nope. The more I tried to pin down the face of the Mystic, the more abstract it became. In the end, the discernable aspects are nearly invisible.

Light, reflection, subtle pattern, expansive white space. My struggle to capture dimensional coattails of the Mystic became woven into my expression of its elusiveness. More than once, I imagined that if I'd translated the painting into a piece of music, it might get closer to what I was after…

The small blue painting is the secret hiding on the back of the canvas. It's an etched list of famous singers who suffer(ed) from terrible, debilitating stage fright. I knew I wanted it to be part of the painting of beauty. It's been ready for a while now. Little did I know, it's part of a totally different painting of the mystic…

The front painting is not the one that took my breath away. That one I was told to paint over, and trust. It's been an epic battle since painting over it. I have not re-captured that mesmerizing, astonishing work. I was lost in that beautiful thing, in a reverie of recognition and calm. A friend who had not seen any of the previous incarnations, and had no clue what to expect, had tears spring to her eyes the minute she saw it. And then, I painted over it.

But this one. This one has had a face appear (not unlike the shroud of turin) that I find unnerving. I don't know what to think. I've been miserable for days, missing my lost painting which captured so much. Left with this one that feels so scary and strange. I captured something, alright. But it's not the side of the mystic that feels so familiar, the one I know like the back of my hand.

Time's up. I'm bewildered. This process I set in motion is really happening, with no clue about deadlines and dates. As it should be. I'm pretty sure there's a HUGE piece of information here. But I haven't quite gotten it unscrambled yet.

~ Lori

In Her Intimacy – Initiations & Gifts

The Mystic's gift is to feel boundless freedom whenever you wish. May the uncharted domains of your life adventure become opportunities to allow this gift of savoring, no longer translating, bridging or giving back. May you feel ease in holding your treasures close, knowing no one will suffer or go for lack. May you experience your heart like this painting, allowing the process of mesmerizement with your own beauty and your own mysticism, then starting all over again to find more of the same through every face and form of yourself and life.

Dreaming

Dream with and as the Mystic... breathing Her alive through you. Doodle. Draw. Jot down your own wisdom from this intimate connection to the multi-faceted nature of your Feminine Soul.

Mother as Artist

The Artist lives in a landscape that precedes vision,
calling worlds into being
from the still point within
- a place she courageously knows as Home.

© JEWELZ ANN LOVEJOY

Passage

The Artist is our guide into the landscape of origination... of all things and ourselves. With Her support we discover the empty spaces that creation is birthed from, and with laser-like focus are able to enter this still point, beckoning forth the fluidity that will bring modes of form and expression into being. To become the Artist, we must enter this stillness, the Great Emptiness, so we can listen with unstructured hearts and undirected spirits to the soundless music of our soul. From here brilliant landscapes become formed. From here harmonies unheard before grow into crescendo and become the sounds of our life. It is our ability to see the Artist within ourselves and ourselves within the deeper wisdom of the Artist that we draw forth endless opportunities to create the landscape of our hearts.

Where will She take you... the artist of yourself? Might She paint a world to your liking filled with the sights, sounds and colors only your heart and soul will recognize? Do you tremble as She stirs deep inside your being? She is there you know, and unavoidable. For as long as you take breath She is the mover behind your movements, the butterfly's fluttering in your chest. She is the hand restoring your richest landscapes, painting you in technicolor even if your perception is black and white. Slow down awhile. Look around at your day. What has she placed in your immediate environment to remind you of your soul stirrings? Are you willing to listen to Her wisdom and truth?

Blessing

I walk with you in to the chambers of your beginnings, and take you farther still to the landscape where no sound, color, music, words or voice can be seen or heard. Here you are deaf, mute, unable to walk, unable to breathe without Her, and don't recognize who you once were. This may frighten parts of you that cling to a name or an identity that wants to know itself only through form. For the Mother as Artist, this is the foundational palette of your greatest discovery. As you allow me to walk you to the threshold of your being before you were, it is here you realize it is all for your innocent choosing. What colors will you pick? What music will you surround yourself with? What landscape will you bring through the eyes of your soul? What utterances will you express to live most deeply into the majesty of life and your most holy creations? I am holding your hand moving it ever so gently. Will you trust this every step of the way? ~ *Mother as Artist*

Prayer

Sacred Mother ~ Beloved Father

Carry me to the threshold of myself, where I can lay down my victimhood and responsibility, and tumble into your care and embrace. May I fall helplessly, voicelessly, as every feeling passes through my heart and any hope for myself. May I surrender deeper into your world, the world of the Mother as Artist. I long to reclaim this part of my soul, this part of my face and being that feels Her guidance always through the brush in my hands, delighting in the strokes She makes now and forevermore. Sacred creation, be with me in the great artistry of my own becoming so I may once again remember I am a Sacred Artist in your life. May all those whose lives I touch feel this gallery of Her beauty, where we look around and see masterpieces of love's delight.

Wisdom

As a woman begins to claim the Artist inside herself, she feels a deeper purpose to her living and actions. Slowly, ever so slowly, the bubbling of creation awakens from deep inside herself and she no longer holds back. At first this might begin with a simple honoring of the mundane moments and things of her day, moving in rhythmic rotation closer and closer within. Eventually a woman who embodies the wisdom and power of the artist begins to revere her every breath and movement, however subtle, of her body, mind and spirit. The Artist as woman cannot separate herself from the moment-to-moment fabric of the sacred. She sees herself as both the weaver and woven. She realizes it is her greatest act to express her own sacredness through all that she does. It is humanity's most precious realization to honor life being birthed through the artistry of the feminine.

The impact on our world of a woman who embodies herself as an Artist transforms every generation from the depths of her pure soul's awakening and pleasure. A woman who moves through her day, aware and celebrating the raising of her children, of the lover she touches and is touched by, of the work and service she gives her heart and self to, is grounding the reality of this preciousness of ourselves. A woman who has sifted through her false perceptions and misgivings to deeply savor her being as a Life Artist, honors the concept that we are sacred as we are. This woman knows that whether she is knitting a scarf, speaking to an audience, laundering diapers, or stirring a pot of simmering stew, she is the life force of creation itself.

Some may frighten at what the Artist claims is
possible, and yet you know and can feel
She is leading you to a brighter way. Hold Her close.
She crafts the colors of your soul around you.

Engagement with the Artist

- Look at the world through the eyes of your womb.

- Watch and listen to children create, play and dream.

- Connect with the Artist and Dreamer within, sketch Her vision.

- Feel all the ways you've downplayed your creative expression. Grieve for the starving, lost Artist within you.

- Grieve for the starving, lost Artists and Creatives in society. Offer words of encouragement and support to those you're inspired by. Validate creativity in our culture.

- Move through a day imagining you're creating a sacred masterpiece... touch, taste, gaze at, and stand before the elements of your world in reverence. At the end of the day, feel what you've created from the fullness of your soul.

- Host an Art gathering. Ask everyone to bring some type of personal sacred expression. Lay out the items and walk around taking in the limitless nature, silliness and awe of what we each have to share.

- Create an artistic piece to express yourself as the Artist.

- Say this within your heart, "I am a Mother. I am an Artist."

- Nurture the qualities of creativity, play, surrender, and being a vessel of life's sacred expression.

Artist Insight & Offerings

The greatest reward is the arrival and participation, and my follow through, offering the best of my ability to experience this pleasure.

~ Jewelz, our Artist

It was such a magnitude of longing to open the crusted layer of my childhood self as the Mother as Artist and Painter.

This gift of painting came through my temple of relation, servitude, humility and ceremony. Every time learning to deeply love myself first. Through this love of self my connection and time between the worlds slowed down as I made love with the Artist as a Painter, connecting with canvas, colors, brushes, vision, prayer, weaving a tapestry of my hidden world within. I was revealed, exposed, witnessed by Her.

The ceremony I'd use to begin painting was to sing open my energies with prayer, and then two hours of journaling. I used the "Crystal Deva" cards by Cindy Watlinhton for encouragement, seeing me further into this experience. With each session the paint colors would jump out. I have three favorite brushes and used recycled cheese tubs and glass jars for cleaning my brushes. I surrounded myself with old towels and an apron.

My favorite time was working in the evening 7pm – 10:30pm at my art studio and sanctuary, when the building was empty and the insulation brought a quietness that soothed my own tucked away place. This was not about home or family responsibilities that could distract me from this intimate time with myself. I loved music softly playing in the background – something that would harmonize and invoke the support of prayer and devotion of painter with me, Jewelz as a dance, a celebration of my heart art life.

I am a novice artist painter. I am thrilled to be right here alongside one another in this exhilarating moment between time and space on our lifeline. By design I am grateful and happy to be asked to choose this Artist's path. I am held in such grace of the mountain highs and valley lows as we are of ever-greater service to our colleagues, friends, our families and our communities. I affirm through my whole holy self that Mother as Artist is building a better world, improving our working environments, and shifting our lives into a precious vision of color, lines, portals of depth on all layers being asked to share and invite to join in the fun.

~ Jewelz

There is always going to be more to share...
~ Jewelz Ann LoveJoy

In Her Intimacy – Initiations & Gifts

The gift of the Artist sets us free to listen to our joy, creative inner folds and wild spirit. May you allow this blessing to support deeply slowing down into the place between and beyond time, space and responsibilities. May you feel aliveness and colors of life being born through you as you show up to a sensual intimacy and love affair with the Artist within. The Artist's prayer is that you take your craft seriously and lightly. That you allow your life to become sacred artistry, and by doing so, provide yourself with the template to express your deepest truth, magic and joy through the medium of a core of self-love.

Dreaming

Dream with and as the Artist... breathing Her alive through you. Doodle. Draw. Jot down your own wisdom from this intimate connection to the multi-faceted nature of your Feminine Soul.

Mother as Healer

As we engage with the Mother as Healer, we enter the domain of who we are in our greatest possibility. She brings us to the breaking wave and offers the softened clarity of our essential wellness, intact no matter how hard the storm hits or how much of ourselves the ocean washes away.

© KRISIEY SALSA

Passage

In the artistry of the Healer we experience a renewed understanding of the purpose of our illnesses and injuries, our hurts, misunderstandings and pain.

The Mother as Healer allows us to enter the ocean of our life, feeling all aspects of ourselves and experiences, and holding our hands out in remembrance that we are never alone, nor separate from the healing capacities that lie within. In reaching out to the Healer within, we navigate our challenges and joys with deepened presence, becoming true and authentic to our inherent wisdom and self. Naturally, as we come closer to Her reality, we let go more and more of the need or desire for anything that attempts to 'fix' or change us, or even that which tries to transform our lives. We begin to embody a deeper presence of the ancient stirrings of our soul in its healed origination. In the hands of the Healer, the ongoing steps and moments of our life become not hurdles or even growth points. They become another creative opportunity to express our true power, presence and surrendered strength to unify our soul with the Face of Her in our deepest health.

Blessing

I come to you in your lost and distorted moments, offering a deeper, more expanded vision of who you are and what is possible. As you contract into fear or uncertainty, believing you are unworthy, unhealthy, unholy, I ride in on the ocean's waves to remind you that in my embrace you are well and never separate from the wholeness you come from. Like a child, so often you kick and scream, refusing to believe I love you, and that I am here for you. Yet I am and always will be. I am the voice, the whisper on the wind, the gentlest touch of a mother's hand caressing a fevered brow, proclaiming you are well, you are loved, you are going to make it through. ~ *Mother as Healer*

Prayer

Beloved Creation ~ Beloved Creator

I enter this space of your heart knowing you welcome me like a child every time. In my innocence I ask to touch and experience the true face of the Healer – the true power of the Mother in Her potent vision of life. Guide me through the caverns of my false projections and misunderstandings about health and well-being. Teach me what is most essential to the artistry of healing, of allowing forth your sacred reality to emerge through my days and me. Through all my interactions and moments, may I call upon you... to hold me, holding myself, in the image of love's beauty, health and grace. In your arms I am Healer and Healed, joining the seemingly two together in sacred unity and service so all those whose lives I touch may know themselves in the face of Her non-shattering love.

Wisdom

When a woman sees herself as a healer, she's opened a doorway in to the deeper stirrings of her inherent feminine wisdom. Healing gifts then arise through a

form that is right and true for her. As a woman allows this internal healing and self transformation to arise, her life becomes the lived artistry of natural experience, flowing through the present moment to serve all she encounters from her own presence and self-healing. Every moment becomes an opportunity to re-envision and realize all the ways she's misconstrued her own reality and claimed health was bestowed from the outside.

As a woman unifies the healer and mother within, seeing one inside of the other, any activities with her community, family, children and self become an act of global transformation and well-being. What she is thinking, how and why she is doing what she does, becomes elevated to the vital role it inherently is – a social and passionate act of justice and wellness for the greater good of humanity.

A woman can allow the healing wisdom of the mother within to guide her into uncharted, foreign territory, to be able to intuitively know what would be the most healing action, remedy or situation to pursue. When a woman values and acknowledges her healing gifts, the world experiences the truth of our lives. As a woman cooks a meal, changes a diaper, makes love to her partner, receives money, and shares her wisdom in the world, immense healing is taking place. Love is transmitted and imbued. A natural order is being restored. Authentic balance is arising. Through becoming a mother (of children, ideas, organizations, projects, communities) a woman is initiated into an ancient healing wisdom – how to move with and as creation itself – bringing life forth and serving it with her ferocious and yielding heart. A Mother births the Healer as herself.

Embodying the Mother as Healer creates a dramatic shift in a woman's life so her choices can reflect the deeper empowerment of her own wisdom, knowing, well-being and courage.

Engagement with the Healer

- When you experience illness, confusion or injury, connect with your inherent wisdom and heed its guidance.

- Connect with plants and flowers in your local area. Create something from them based on your intuition (*If guided to ingest or take plants internally, know with 100% certainty the safety and edibleness of each plant).

- List qualities you perceive in a Healer. Write down all the ways you've experienced these qualities in yourself.

- Speak or sing out loud, "I am the face of the Healer". Notice how this feels and what wisdom comes forth.

- Dress as a Healer, noting the colors and fabrics you are drawn to.

- Create a 'healing recipe' for yourself... for a meal or how you will spend your day. Notice what you are drawn to for foods and activities when you honor yourself as the Healer of your life.

- Offer healing support to someone in need. Trust yourself and what you share.

- Connect with the trees and forest.

- Create an artistic piece to express yourself as a Healer.

- Ask your inner healer what to do in each circumstance.

Artist Insight & Offerings

The Healer...

I took a walk with the healer for 45 days and nights.
I followed in her footsteps.
Her exhale became my inhale.
I wanted to be her, to suck her essence into my bones, my being.
Maybe then I could heal myself, heal loved ones, heal the world.

We danced ~ danced with wild abandon.
Soul shaking shifting occurred.
She led and I followed.
She embraced me and I wept.
She spoke and I listened...

I am YOU ~
In you
From you
For you
By you
Full of you.

Beauty FULL you.

~ Krisiey, our Healer

In Her Intimacy – Initiations & Gifts

The Healer's gift is that Her wisdom keeps growing through you, to express and portray the miracle of our world. It is rare to see and show the immense beauty of what is right before us and within us. The Healer's prayer is for this to continue to become your living reality... *forever* seeing the immense beauty that is right within you. "I am YOU. In you. From you. For you. By you. Full of you. Beauty FULL you." May your heart be forever opened to the sun's light, and your arms surrendered to the mystery of creation.

Dreaming

Dream with and as the Healer... breathing Her alive through you. Doodle. Draw. Jot down your own wisdom from this intimate connection to the multi-faceted nature of your Feminine Soul.

Mother as Distiller

The woman who is ready and willing to engage with this aspect of the Mother will come to know the unbreakable faith she contains within.

Passage

To be imbued by the Distiller is an act of courageous humility. She will not be found in the seeking, but rather, in the surrender. Her grace is not understood by the mind or the concepts we hold about love. Like the fire that burns and disintegrates, creating ash from all that was, to engage with the Distiller takes our greatest humbling, faith and conviction. As we experience the power of Her commitment to our potential realized, we fear less and less the pathway of transformation we encounter and will create as we rediscover and uncover our deepest truth. The process of distillation in our culture has been depicted with a mighty hand. It is frightening, and most have run from it. Yet all that dissolves away as we experience the tender transformation of the feminine, who wishes not through her unbounded tears to harm in any way, is always for our best. We can breathe in this sacred reality, in which to transform we need not hurt or be harmed, force or be forced, dominated or domineering. Through the Distiller we uncover a face of love few have seen in this life for its been shrouded in misconstrual and misunderstanding. To directly and intimately connect with the Distiller awakens a completely new foundation within one's soul. The dawn of a new day in which growth and change need not come from a path of suffering or disembodiment, but one of complete renewal in the sweetness of Her motherly embrace.

Blessing

I will show you the essence of yourself, the true importance of all you have and will experience, and of your relations. To be with me means dissolution of all you've believed prior about who you are and what love is. You cannot discover me if you're not willing to let me lead the way. You will not see my face if you always think you know my or your own form. To be with me can feel like death, only for as long as you see straight through your concepts of life. I am the face of the divine force that will reveal reality to and through you, as you allow your perceived limitations to be embraced in my love. Your humanity, your fear, doubts, and uncertainties, all guide you to me – to the Face of the Distiller. Like mashing down fruit to make jam, I reform and refine your understandings of yourself and true sweetness, so you may be reformed and reborn with all of love's almighty ingredients. To be distilled by Her Grace removes nothing from one's source. It only breaks it down so the bond and sacred connection is more readily noticed and digested. I am the willingness that knows your most essential gifts, essence, love and form can never be destroyed, only remade in Her alchemy of Re-creation. ~ *Mother as Distiller*

Prayer

Sacred Life ~ Holy Death

Take me before the Face of the Distiller so I might discover myself. Even in my fear of losing all I have known and all I have loved, help me reach out and hold my Mother's hand – the unbreakable sacred connection that only and always has my greatest intentions and joy intact in Her own. I cannot live in the limited ideas I have held about my life and self anymore. Show me the gifts in my prior ways of living so I might continually refine my capacity to love. Distill all parts of my life experience into the golden ash of divine resurrection so my soul may be richly restored and able to deeply nourish the lives and legacy of all those I shall meet. I want to know the essence of myself in Her name, and live from this always. I long to know the essence of you and of love. Enact through me the sacred power of distillation so in each moment I may walk with arms outstretched, truly sharing your essential nourishment with all of life. Thank you. Amen.

Wisdom

In our culture the Distiller has taken on a frightening role. Who wants to let all they are and have known turn to ash? Who wants to willingly give themselves into the fire?

The woman who is ready and willing to engage with this aspect of the Mother will come to know the unbreakable faith she contains. This element of our process into the deeper places of our soulful being knows no limits to what we can and will face or go through. The woman who allows the Distiller to work through her, cares not what will happen, knowing there is nothing she can't face from the power of her own presence. This brings a startling sense of freedom, assurance and clarity to live life fully.

What if we taught this to our children, drew this out through our mothers, respected this in our men? What if we welcomed one another and ourselves into the arms of complete dissolution?

What if we were encouraged to live in a constant state of surrender in to the arms that deeply support us?

The feminine fire of our nature is entwined with this Distillation process. We cannot access the immensity, power, subtlety and presence of this part within ourselves if we do not let outer circumstances demolish all we have known and believed was important. Without engaging with the distillation of our lives, we may never come to know what *really* matters. We may remain in a whirlwind of following endless notions of what we have been told and been falsely telling ourselves.

If and when a woman is willing to enter the fires of her dissolution, she'll be greeted by a mighty hand, one that aids her to unfailingly turn the ashes of her life into a striking beauty never before seen or known. Such creations do not come from this world.

As a mother grows intimate with the power of the Distiller, she faces every circumstance within her, her children and family's life with an assurance that this world rarely affirms or confers. It comes through her own navigation of the creation that lives within her being, from a world that lives beyond and before all of this. Here a woman finds she is always holding hands with that which loves her beyond it all.

The woman who allows the Distiller to work through
her, cares not what will happen, knowing there is nothing
she can't face from the power of her own presence.

Engagement with the Distiller

- Create and tend a fire. Offer it items and expressions of cherished parts of your past that you know are ready to transform. Watch.

- Commune and talk with ash. Create something from it.

- Till ash into your garden and soil. Offer it to a favorite nature land spot in ceremony.

- Visit a volcanic area.

- Go to where a forest fire has been.

- Bring innocence and play to working with fire. Notice your edges around safety.

- Talk to the sun. Let its rays teach you about the burning and passion of love and your commitment to growth.

- Write down your favorite ways to grow, and your most tender ways to change and transform.

- Spend time by the stove, boiling things to watch the process and see what occurs.

- Create an artistic piece to express yourself as the Distiller

- Say this within your heart, "I am a Mother. I am a Distiller"

- Make jam.

Artist Insight & Offerings

Standing here, I really see that love is where my heart is,
where my loves are.
We are the ground we stand on.
It's not my things, my house, my street, none of that.
We are it wherever we are, however we are.

~ SARAH, OUR DISTILLER

1st sketch: Mother Distiller is fire (sun) in the sky (air) with thick curls of reds oranges yellows. There is joy in the sorrow, the knowing of the message distilled... tears (hot salty water) into a pool/lake of blues greens whites (moon) creating the symbol of infinity with a cross-section of a smaller lemniscate (love, friendship, relationship).

It's pretty amazing. I wake thinking about it, almost like dreaming. The image is getting clearer and clearer. I hope I can bring the image forward through this (my) body.

And then there was a fire... Sarah came home in September 2013, about 1/3 of the way through our process, to find her stove had malfunctioned. This resulted in smoldering and smoke throughout her house, and prompted a 6-week journey of moving her family from place to place while their home was cleaned and eventually repainted. In this process she explored her commitments to herself and what was most important to her life... a distillation occurred. What follows are her realizations during this journey into embodying the Distiller...

What I see today is that my reality is not Reality. What has been perceived by me as 'hard' or 'scary' or 'unsettling' or 'ungrounded' is all illusion based on perception. What actually is – what IS – is Love.

We are so routine-oriented that to be pulled out of our home and have no routine has really shaken us. I began a story today in my mind called, "When there's no where to go". The concept of Nothing (where anything is possible) is really up against the concept of nothing like a black hole of despair. Or some such thing. The constant trying (at anything) is exhausting. There is no try! There is only do! The constant running away from thoughts or feelings or commitments... is also exhausting. And when there's nowhere to go but here... what is left? Not truth. Truth doesn't exist either! Inside that nothing, there is what we create as a possibility.

Love is forever and ever and all of the noise is just a storm (it might destroy things, hurt – what do we expect? It's a storm!) It too will pass; it's just for now. Love is forever and always. There is always someone loving me – at this very moment! – right here on Earth. And there is always the Love of heaven. Always.

Return again, return again. Return to the land of your soul. I'm hurting pretty bad right now with tiredness and upset caused by tiredness and sore feelings of constantly being challenged. This fall has been walloping. I wonder if it will ever stop. I constantly remind myself that it doesn't have to feel hard, and I am just exhausted. I want to hibernate like a bear. I want to hide. I want it to be easier. And I remember that easier is actually the going through it – the not giving up.

The only things I am truly focused on right now have to do with the right here and right now.

~ SARAH

I am not bringing to life this project in any other form than this love, this family, these children, putting this house back together *newly*, finding rhythm in this transitional space.

~ SARAH PAGE

In Her Intimacy – Initiations & Gifts

The Distiller's gift is that you know nothing more is needed... what you have given is enough. May your body allow the deepest rest and restoration. If you wish, may you wake each day knowing nothing is needed beyond loving what you love with the fullness of your ease, with the grace of your truth, with the integrity of being you and living as such. May your fire soar into the sky, witnessing through falling tears this infinite beauty of your being that can never be captured, only lived through each of your moments as you.

I have nothing further to offer than what has already been given.

~ SARAH PAGE

Dreaming

Dream with and as the Distiller... breathing Her alive through you. Doodle. Draw. Jot down your own wisdom from this intimate connection to the multi-faceted nature of your Feminine Soul.

❧ Mother as Decomposer

The Mother as Decomposer reveals to us our glory through all we've been and all we shall be, leaving no stone unturned or aspect of ourselves at the wayside.

© HOLLY HINSON

Passage

To witness the power of the Decomposer in oneself is an act of death and of rebirth. It is discovering the point within where duality and opposition cease to pull one's spirit outward or away. It is an ancient place of presence awakening to see angels in our demons and new life in all we've attempted to destroy. The blessings of the Decomposer do not fit into any of our notions about the way life works, for inherent in this wisdom and power is a knowing that life is created from breaking everything down and giving it over... offering it to the earth, the soil, the land below our feet and the air around our bodies... all symbolizing the embodiment of the Mother. The Mother as Decomposer reveals to us our glory through all we've been and all we shall be, leaving no stone unturned or aspect of ourselves at the wayside. She picks up every parcel and piece of our own discarded sense of self, bringing it into her embrace to be turned into precious humus for our soul's garden to blossom.

Blessing

Follow me daughter. Be not afraid. I take you in to the deepest existence... into your own dark fertility... into places within that are untouched by anything of this world, where no light has ever shined. Did you know it is here you will find me... it is here you will find your own renewal? Here you will discover the capacity to be reborn through me... into and through Her eternal love. As a flower blossom at the end of its display of colorful glory trusts its decay, its drying out, its incessant thirst, as simply one stage of its perpetual radiance and expression, I invite you to trust this, to trust the decomposition. I invite you here into the folds of my darkness. It is here the womb of the heart truly thrives. I imbue the ground, your foundations, with new vitality and nutrients each time you come to me, laying down all you've grown, harvested, planted, tended... and loved. Come daughter. Come closer. Offer up all you've seen of creation more glorious than you ever deemed possible. Lay down all you've taken intense pleasure in and trust me to decompose the essence of your joy into a new seedbed that'll blossom in tomorrow's springtime. My love for you can be hard to understand. Turn not away. I love you with my whole being and have offered to exist beyond what is pleasant and comfortable for you so as to hold and whisper remembrance of your own brilliance even in the blackness of your darkest night.
~ *Mother as Decomposer*

Prayer

Ancient Land ~ Holy Earth

Take me into my dark fertility – to the places I rarely go or trust myself to behold the sacred face of Decomposition. Show me the many ways I hold back from complete surrender into my most primordial joy. How can I know who I am unless I release all I've been? Guide me through the landscape I have filled with my ghosts and my own betrayal – to discover a deeper pleasure within myself and of Her love. I long to fear nothing of true life, knowing Her hand tills all beauty beyond what I can comprehend. May I be a beacon for others still distrusting, still holding back. Help me fall into Her blackness – into a world I cannot see or perceive. Remind me I am held here. Remind me She is here with me. Remind me love is waiting, always willing, showing me towards a new horizon and a new day. May I discover an otherworldly trust within, prompting me on and onward still, even when I see not a hand before my face. Through Her power as Decomposer may my life's legacy become fertile ground for all those who walk beside me now and always. Thank you. Amen.

Wisdom

Those familiar with thrusting their hands deep into the rich soil of the earth know there are worlds upon worlds below ground. Those who sit quietly, gazing upon the smallest area below their feet, understand thriving cultures of life exist right before our eyes.

To work with the Decomposer takes slowness of heart, akin to the rhythms of a babe growing in the womb. Movements are beckoned from connection of oneself to another as a single unit. This is what occurs as a woman works with this quality within. Her hand's movement becomes the life of her heart's expression. She realizes all things work together to create the Mother's beauty, bounty, wonder and joy.

A woman who travels and remains here in the embrace of her own internal darkness, running not from the terrorizing or uncomfortable places we all must one day face, learns to trust not just herself, but the entire Universe through her. She sees and feels how there is nothing to stop what is to come to be. She learns to move with instead of against it, finding immense beauty in her heartache, loneliness, in loss and futility, in her aging and ultimately by her grace. The woman who's directly met and embraced the face of the Decomposer is as real as it comes. She's opened to the power of her heart, body and soul being broken open and down, so the most potent seeds of her life may take root and grow.

Through the pregnancy and birth process, a woman is naturally initiated by the Decomposer. This is the wisdom of transformation. In this process a mother learns to give her body over for something beyond what she could ever imagine or contain in her mind's limitations. She opens to revelations of oneness and unity, of dissolution and letting go. A mother learns the gift of surrender through birth as the Decomposer brings her intimately into Her overseeing embrace.

It is important to name our fears when calling upon the Decomposer. We bring them to the surface, one by one, with the tenderest embrace of a mother holding each of her beloved children. The Mother as Decomposer does not separate our joys from our fears. As we enter the landscape of the Decomposer, we feel ourselves existing beyond such definitions and limitations.

In our society we live in constant fear of our own decomposition... of the decay of ourselves and everything around us. If we chose to embrace this falling away, dying and disintegrating, we'd become resolute with the power of the universe working with, for and because of us, on our behalf. We've created a culture now steeped in fighting against the natural progression as we work at the speed of light and place all those people and situations that are too slow to keep up, away from the mainstream.

Eventually the Decomposer catches up to us all. When we hold Her gifts close and learn to see their power, beauty and wisdom within ourselves, our world as we've known it grows a new face, more exquisite than we could ever imagine.

Lay down all you've taken intense pleasure in and trust
me to decompose the essence of your joy into a new
seedbed that'll blossom in tomorrow's springtime...

Engagement with the Decomposer

- Work with the compost bin as sacred life art

- Stand before compost. Breathe in its living expression. Circulate its wisdom through your system.

- Till soil. Feel this on the inner plane. Notice your body and breath.

- Till your womb space by rubbing and kneading your belly. What's going on?

- Spread composted material and manure around your land/scaping. Offer it in prayer and notice your body.

- Play with soil and in the layers of earth.

- Dig a hole as deeply as you can. Watch it over time.

- Find an earthen cave and get in. Commune and listen to the inside of the earth.

- Cover yourself with sand at the beach. Rest. Feel.

- Say to yourself, "I am a Mother. I am the Decomposer."

- Create an artistic piece to express yourself as the Decomposer.

- Be with the dying/transitioning (with a person transitioning, a plant withering, an animal passing on). Notice how you engage.

- Write a letter to your dying self. Acknowledge all the things your heart and soul wish to say.

Artist Insight & Offerings

*I pushed through my own darkness and
came out of it with wings.
For without darkness, there is no light.*

~ HOLLY, OUR DECOMPOSER

This has been an incredible journey – a roller coaster of experiences, emotions, and breakthroughs. This project has touched me on a deep level and continues to guide me through my innermost being – cradling the child, the mother, the woman. I feel such gratitude for being a part of this – my heart swells.

This whole process has been such a gift. Pushing and pulling and diving deep.

This has been a year of great growth for me. I feel that I'm emerging from a cocoon, and while that sounds beautiful, it's also been very painful in the way great growth and emergence can be. Many things came up for me in this project – self doubt and a strong need to feel in control were recurring throughout. When I finished the piece, I wasn't sure how I felt about it. It felt too... precise. I realized that I work so hard to put on that very face while feeling the opposite, not allowing that inner chaos to be seen. That because I've felt such a lack of control in my life, I have trouble letting go of control when given the option. I've always envisioned myself a free spirit, but I'm finding that's not necessarily the case. But in my own way, I did allow myself to feel and follow my intuition with the decomposer. I went about it in a different way, and I'm working on accepting my true self – releasing disappointment I feel when I don't live up to the grand and unrealistic (and unauthentic) expectations I have for myself. So when I release the judgment, I look at my work and truly do feel that it's a touching reflection of the Mother as Decomposer.

Initially, I felt darkness with the decomposer. It's interesting how bright the piece turned out. It's a layered piece, and I found a healing in each layer. It speaks to me in a very special way.

The timing of all of this blows my mind, as all I have been through with this piece has been a direct reflection of what's going on in my life.

This piece is a collection of five paintings combined into one.

I found myself feeling a darkness with the decomposer, and initially painted layers of darkness – browns, reds, and golds – on paper. While painting, I found the first strokes to be pure – the truth. And as I layered on, the pureness and truth began to get smudged and foggy until the truths were no longer obvious as they became distorted with darkness.

I then cut that painting up, as I had a vision to surround the darkness in gold – there's beauty to the darkness. In cutting that painting up, I felt the decomposition – the breaking down, the letting go...

I then painted the woman's silhouette on canvas, and had a vision to have a bright light surrounding her, as well as a brightness emanating from within. The butterflies were the last component. I wasn't sure how I wanted to finish her, and so I began painting scenes on other pieces of paper – clouds in a blue sky, colors in a garden, pure golden light – and found that the light sprang from the darkness. And so I was called to give those paintings wings...

~ HOLLY

I'm working on accepting my true self – releasing disappointment
I feel when I don't live up to the grand and unrealistic
(and unauthentic) expectations I have for myself.

~ HOLLY HINSON

In Her Intimacy – Initiations & Gifts

The Decomposer's gift is giving permission for the full range of you to shine. May the tumbling stones and the fluttering butterflies bless you. Each day may your body breathe in and receive such beauty, light, power and strength. May you look forever upon yourself for the gift that you are, and have been to us all. May you prowl in the darkness and dance in the light.

Dreaming

Dream with and as the Decomposer... breathing Her alive through you. Doodle. Draw. Jot down your own wisdom from this intimate connection to the multi-faceted nature of your Feminine Soul.

Mother as Midwife

The gift of the Midwife is knowing all that comes through us is truly of benefit for humanity.

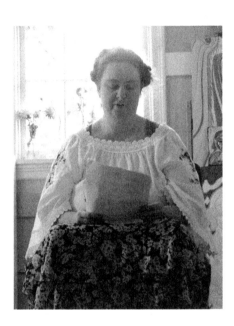

Passage

The Midwife comes close to our side as we move through the transitions of our lives. Her power is being ever-present, holding steady and clear vision of our potential and what is natural and organic in and through our lives. She knows what we can achieve and holds the space open for us to move through the course at our own pace, in our own way, never losing site of the wish to birth and bring forward the greatest in ourselves and through all our creations. The Mother as Midwife will not meddle, manipulate or force a chosen outcome. She is there to support us fully facing each step of the journey so we may make impassioned choices moving us toward our own glory – the glory within coming forth and through to bless the world. The Midwife within our being resists not our tears or tantrums... our detours or devastations. She sees through all our outbreaks and heartbreaks to the potential for rebirth within us that is ever present, within all, within each women. The Midwife will not walk our path for us, yet will instead look us deeply in the eyes when we believe we've gone astray or can't take one step further. It is then She proclaims, "...just one breath, and one breath more. You can do it. Breathe. It's all it takes." The Midwife understands the process of our birth and remains in servitude to its ultimate beauty and simplicity. She is ever assured.

Blessing

Beloved Angel, I am here by your side cheering you on – not towards a predetermined victory, but towards the birth of your Divine Self and sacred innocence. I call the babe forth from the womb and know what it takes to bring Her here. I know you will face death one hundred times over. I will hold your hand each step of the way. I will wipe your brow when the inner fire of your being has scorched all surfaces you've prior taken nourishment from. And when you fall down and can't go on, I won't pick you up. I will stand by your side knowing you have the power and love within you to move – to allow the Spirit of your being to caress your soul and teach you to stand and fly. Sacred Daughter, you are the Mother of all Creation. I am a guidepost that cherishes your innate capacities to go for it, again and again, creating from the inner cauldron of your deepest being. I treasure the gifts of yourself you have yet to know would appear each time you cried out. I love you as the rain adores each blossom, quenching its thirst when it feels it cannot grow in the midday heat another moment more. Oh sweet child, fall into my arms and let me hold you in your agony, your uncertainty, in death's grave. My arms cradle you until you are refreshed, ready to take in another gift from the heavens within your soul, to rebirth as the child, as the mother, as the lover in the sanctity of your heart's ripeness. Let me walk this life with you at each turn and corner. Together we may reveal the capacity for all life to be reborn through our partnership and love. ~ *Mother as Midwife*

Prayer

Divine Mother ~ Innocent Child

Hold me now at your breast and remind me of the pathway that brought me here, from within the power of all creation that birthed my life forth. Guide me through the dark caverns of my denial, through the endless deaths of myself, into your care each step of the way. I know I cannot and do not birth my self on my own. Yet I know I must hold the conviction from deep within my being, that no one else can do this for me. I am the choice point that calls out, calling you forth to my aide when I know I cannot take another step in any direction but towards my own rebirth. Be with me Holy Midwife. Let me listen to what you feel I am capable of. Let me feel the power you hold in belief of what I can do. Let me feel your presence when I've gone to the edge of what I can withstand, crying out for a pause, for a new pathway to unfold. Hold me Mother as the glory of your own reflection, and as the glory of what is created thus forth. I offer my brow to be christened at your care. With you by my side, I am the Mother – I am the Child. Birth me through your steady gaze that witnesses a process of ever-unfurling creation so I may share with all of life the original joy of being formed by such love. Thank you. Amen.

Wisdom

In our culture, Midwifery is presently resided over by agencies that determine legalization, certification and training. The work of Midwives is not to be underestimated, nor devalued for growing, professionalizing or advancing with the times. Yet this move towards external accreditation reflects a rampant societal fear in our inherent capacity to show up fully through the process of life, birth and death. We've become afraid to aid through our meekest and most powerful presence. In addition to the legalization of midwifery for creating core standards and healthy adherences, there is also a belief we are not enough as we are, nor can we be what another most needs through their passage of initiation. We've conditioned ourselves to fear that we actually *might know* what to do and when to do it. We've doubted our internal capacity to be the most powerful resource to another as they move through life's transitions. This reflects our underlying assumption that we are not worthy or capable of receiving this in our own hour of need. The inherent proclamation of the Midwife states, "Support will be by your side as you require it!"

The journey of reclaiming the Mother as Midwife requires our power, love and instinctual wisdom. As a woman 'presses her brow' to the ground of the earth in surrender, she lets the Mother symbolically christen her, learning what true service is. This is the initiation of the Midwife: to remain in tune with what is most needed and offer this through her resources of self, training, medical tools and support. Whatever a woman has within and around her to provide safe passage for literal and spiritual birthing will be used through trusting the Midwife within. This is symbolic for us as we make our way through our own life cycles, allowing new life and aspects of ourselves forth.

One of the gifts of a mother who has engaged with the Midwife within, is to know when *not* to step in... to stand by another's side and let them navigate their self-initiation. This aspect of our transformation will present through as many forms and faces as there are human beings on the planet. The Midwife within us is the living force that honors the passage of another... to face what she must, to feel what he must, to come to her own realizations as only she can. A Midwife trusts this. She learns to stand at the edge, letting another take center stage. She knows this passage is a woman's to take. She listens and honors, being there when needed, stepping back and away even in the hardest moments. A Midwife will not discredit a mother's own power. In the end this is the only awakening that truly matters. This is what the Midwife within us commits to as we come home to the journey of our life and the organic birthing of our soul. We welcome the experience and wisdom of the Midwife within. We become this living force for ourselves and all others.

Just one breath, and one breath more. You can do it. Breathe. It's all it takes.

Engagement with the Midwife

- Show up for another in your rawness, truth and presence.

- Trust the Universe to work through you. Sense when to step forth and when to rest.

- Notice when you doubt yourself and your capacity to 'be enough'.

- Look in a mirror and state, "Just one breath. And one breath more. You can do this. Breathe. It's all it takes."

- Hold another's hand in their darkest hour.

- Ask someone to hold *your* hand in your deepest vulnerability.

- Spend time with newborn babes. Ask them how they got here. Trust the ensuing conversation.

- Be present to the transitions (birth, death, life, rebirth).

- Make a list of the qualities of a Midwife. Put a star next to the ones you contain.

- Say within yourself, "I am a Mother. I am a Midwife." Breathe. Feel.

- Create an artistic expression of and with the Midwife.

- Work with moving below your judgments of self, life and the way things go – yours and others.

- When someone is crying, be present. Allow the crying to unfold without trying to fix or change anything. Allow another to do this for you. Show up to do this for yourself.

Artist Insight & Offerings

I wanted it to be "right." I wanted perfection. HA!

I had a dream last night, I woke up crying. Because someone in my dream, who I once knew, who lived in what I called a paradise, recognized ME and said, "Oh, it's YOU!" And then I wrote and wrote and wrote. And then I listened to your (Sharon's) anchoring voice and so many of the words I had written... shell, shadow, light... came up in your voice and I was shocked! We are aligned... and I think all of us are aligned who are working on this project. I wanted something that would last – a visual art piece. I thought poetry wasn't important. HA! I thought my singing was so fleeting... that it wouldn't last but as a wind passing by. I wanted to be remembered. Then I remembered that 'I am important' and what 'I do is important.' I write poetry and sing songs. This is who I am and distilled... it is me. I am searching right now. It is so hard to listen to my guiding voice when so many voices are calling to me for help. But if I carve out time for myself, I can hear the voice... barely.

There will be something for you at the end. And it will not be perfect... but it will be me!

~ ANNA, OUR MIDWIFE

The Face of the Mother: Midwife

I. YOU

Every person, every soul
started their first journey
down the birth canal.
Long and winding,
fun or scary—the fear of falling
began with the first yank out.
Yet
midwives wait and watch

and gently help the new ones into being
to take their first breath
in a nurturing place.
It's so simple, you see—
we have so very many journeys in our lives,
and each one can be scary or fun,
but it's better to know that you're not alone
that someone is waiting and watching
and holding your hand
until you emerge
on the other side
and you don't fear falling anymore.

II. OPENING

She reveals to you
what you already know
gives you a hand
says nothing
only looks and sees the beauty that is you
it is a reflection of the goddess
and it almost always makes you cry
Her eyes mirror back your own face
confused in a world of pain
and shows you the certainty: YOU CAN DO THIS
You were made to do this
You exist for this moment
You are the most beautiful thing alive
You are power
You are love
You move the world
literally—you are the world
and your plates shift to make way for a new life

Your mind is a gift—it interprets nerve impulses and decides what
they mean.
It's a tool—YOU are ultimately in control of what it decides.
Yet in the most ironic twist
you must give up control
utterly and completely
to the power of Her within you
for the storm is coming
and you can sit inside your shell and let it pass you by
and you may feel safe
but
you will miss
the glorious clouds
the amazing wind on your face
the earth shaking under your feet.
But the shell is hard
and hard to break
and it hurts oh it hurts
to crack that first crack
for we are well protected, yes
encased in ignorance and fed by our own mother's sweet nectar
a gift without which we would die
and yet
    at some point
        it runs out
            and the only choice left
is
to break free

III. IN FRONT/BEHIND/WITHIN

It is so dark
There is no light
until

you go with Her
and the moon is so big—bigger than you've ever seen it
behind you and in front of you
reflected on the rocks ahead
leading the way
so brilliant
yet so pedestrian
as if She hardly even knows you're there
but
She knows
and She remembers
and She loves
you.
The crossing will be dangerous
but it will be well worth it.
All around life will go on as if it didn't know it
wasn't connected—
but the connections are not for us to know
We must
simply
trust.
She is the reflection of you
on the rock, on the tree, in the pond and through the paths of our lives
when we move, when we stop
She is there.
She leads you down rocky paths you never thought you'd know,
you never thought you'd try
you're walking in darkness
and suddenly She's there
lighting your way—She is within you.
You don't need a car
you can't take a plane, or a boat, nor any combustible engine.
To take a vehicle like that would mean that you miss the actual journey.

Perhaps a sailboat
or a bicycle....
Nevertheless,
You must walk the bumpy road
put one foot in front of the other
and
eventually
you will arrive.

IV. POSTPARTUM

She looks in on you
She is just behind your shoulder
opening your eyes in the morning
after the long sleep
She is there to welcome you to a new day
a new life beginning
fresh and clean
even with all the knowledge of the night
and the lives before
wiping the membranes across your cornea
you push open your eyelids
and let in the light
so bright it hurts
yet you cannot turn back
you cannot make it dark again like it was before.
Now you have the knowing of the sun and the morning.
Here you are.
You have arrived.

~ ANNA

In Her Intimacy – Initiations & Gifts

The Midwife's gift is to continue to expand into the space that values yourself and your own voice. May you feel how sacred your expression is and what healing it brings to others. As you write and sing and offer up your truth and birthing beauty, all of life opens to being supported in the arms of the Mother. She prays you dance to your own song, taking in the healing of your own grace. May your wisdom of the Mother as Midwife stand with you now and always as you birth into yourself again and again.

Dreaming

Dream with and as the Midwife... breathing Her alive through you. Doodle. Draw. Jot down your own wisdom from this intimate connection to the multi-faceted nature of your Feminine Soul.

Mother as Creatress

*On our knees we find ourselves
weeping in gladness...
in realization that we are a vessel to
beauty's birthing,
to love's incarnation,
no matter what.*

© JEWELZ ANN LOVEJOY

Passage

The Creatress carries you forth from the land of the void, through the great passage... onward into the seat of your power as Creator making love with all of life. She holds the wisdom that when you create, *anything* you create and every time, blesses, with no exception. The Mother as Creatress gives you the sanctity to deeply enter the playground of your soul and express its eternal longings through forms of your being. To work with Her is an act of mercy and surrender. Never again will you simply be picking up a pen to write, or dipping a brush in color to paint. Working consciously with the wisdom of the Creatress transforms our understanding of how and why we are doing what we do. Through this sacred partnership, we confront an opportunity to live in an ongoing state of humility. A deep-seated knowing arises each time we say Yes! to being an instrument for creation. Everything we do, say, touch and choose is the calling forth of the Divine. Through the Creatress, one's life becomes a living prayer to all of creation. On our knees we find ourselves weeping in gladness... in realization that we are a vessel to beauty's birthing, to love's incarnation, no matter what. Working with the Mother as Creatress defies any small notions we've held of ourselves. As She arises within we cannot but look in the mirror and discover a living King and Queen.

Blessing

Dearest Daughter, come to me like a babe rooting for her Mother's breast. Drink at my bosom until you feel saturated and fully nourished. Stay as long as you like and let me caress your skin, heart and mind. I am your mother, your sister, and your friend. You are my child and my own face. From the same love you were created by, will you find the pathway for resurrecting your own sacred creations, always in connection to me and your fullest life. Follow me until the lines are blurred and you no longer find the Source of your beauty and power anywhere outside of you. Feel your Source deeply lodged within your own self, your own womb of being. I am the prayer that returns you to this rightful and restful repose in the bosom of your soul. Here you remember that all which flows from you is holy – your blood, visions, desires and grief. This is all sacred ground for the great work of love to shine through. Angel of my life, you are the hands, body, wisdom and face that bring my power into form. Sacred Creatress, you are here to sing the Heavens home. ~ *Mother as Creatress*

Prayer

Dearest Calling Forth ~ Wondrous Void From Which All Arises

I turn to you now, stripped bare and reborn, longing only to use myself for this glorious expression of love, in the immaculate dance of life. Show me where I cling to notions of being unworthy. Show me how I resist your power working through my own being. Show me how hiding my light is a great disservice to all. I wish to work with you in the power, love and beauty of all creation. I wish to see my face as your own so I might remember and reflect the same wherever I go, and with whomever I am with. What will it take for me to come as close to you as I can, to allow my life and work to be a gift of your sacred expression? What will it take to never again hold anything back? I wish to give all that I am and all that I have into the creation of love, into the never-ending story of life. Use me Divine Creatress to free this land and these people. Use me to free my own soul. May I truly walk in humility and surrender – accepting how deeply my gifts are needed and how important my purpose is. To this truth I open my heart. For this truth I live and breathe. Thank you. Amen.

Wisdom

As the Mother as Creatress awakens through a woman, she rewrites her story and repaints her living reality. Like the spider weaving a daily web, a woman learns to discover freshness within, repurposing herself through her moments and actions. What once was something chosen simply 'to do', now becomes seen through the eyes of love's vitality pulsing outward to nourish and bless all that will exist.

Our lives are richly engrained with the knowing of sacred incarnation as the Creatress takes root inside. No longer do we fear our own unworthiness. We learn to face it each time, turning inward for the greatest embrace, knowing this frees everyone in moving more closely to their own soul's calling.

For the one willing to embody the Creatress, she lives into and through every possibility and color of the spectrum. Each time the seedling of potential releases from her inner womb space, she gradually allows its natural unfolding. The process of life's

birth through her power takes shape as she watches creation's own longing to give of itself with love.

The mother who engages with the Creatress allows a masterpiece to be born from her listening. Following her need for rest and quietude, flowing with her own natural rhythms, trust and wonder, she learns what she is made of. In this landscape a woman neither forces nor resists the union and harmonizing that occurs each time creation is born.

In allowing the gifts of the Creatress, we come in to balance in our own being, working with the full landscape of our powers of creation and destruction, of light and dark, of our masculine and feminine. Being with the Creatress signifies a return to our maturity and our innocence. We are present to the full range of emotions, leaving no stone unturned, shunning from nothing within or around.

In working with the Creatress' wisdom, a palpable tenderness towards whatever we find in one another and ourselves arises. This enduring stance in our vast and rooted expansion is the doorway in which creativity flows through, winding and weaving, gathering and collecting, undulating and discarding, as life is born and reborn again. The work of the Creatress is underway even when it appears silent, dark, void or still. As we call Her to our aide, She shows us that every aspect, from birth to death and what happens ever after, is a vital stage in creation's fullness. Nothing exists outside of this. Even the uncoiling or unwinding of us is necessary to the reweaving of the next state. The Creatress holds the intricate rhythm, pacing and interconnection of creation's workings together.

*To work with the Creatress means we've passed through
our own conscious cycles and are poised to see and
experience in ourselves Her mode of life's expression.*

Engagement with the Creatress

- Express. Express what lies within. Silence is expression.

- Feel where you're afraid of your birthing power.

- Offer forgiveness, honesty and reconciliation to your inner Creatress.

- Do a gentle yet engaging belly massage as you wake in the morning. Envision clearing your House of Fertility (womb space). Begin your projects here.

- Honor unworthiness. Depict it through creative acts and your vulnerability. Hide not from the tenderness of yourself.

- Allow the Creatress to Mother your dreams.

- Pray outlandishly to feel your Life Artistry. Open to ways your dreams exist and are a part of your life. Claim this validation.

- Create gardens, altars and prayers that honor the visions you hold. Allow them tangible space to be witnessed, seen, touched and celebrated.

- Explore pleasure. What colors, sights, feelings and textures attract you? What feels good on your skin? How do you like to be touched? What sensual and sexual pleasures ignite you? Which ones repel? Feel without judgment or pretense.

- Permit yourself to adore what you do. Create from your sense of satisfaction and pleasure.

- Say within your heart, "I am a Mother. I am the Creatress." Breathe.

- Create an artistic piece to express yourself as the Creatress.

I am the Creatress of these heart songs of my own wellspring.
I am no longer choosing to tend or care for
others in the old ways that I have.
I'm free. I am healed. I am what I am.

~ Jewelz, our Creatress

First only draft, two hours start to finish, watercolor and acrylic.

She is satisfied, a teacher of allowing forgiveness especially around how we weave and yield our power in our world. She is comfortable, seen, well cared for and liked by her creator. With this peace and personal reverence, her magic and mystery changes and reveals itself in the healing of elements, and all water places and sources. It shows itself as a face that can move easily into ethereal connectedness to the invisible spirit as watcher. She who sees us and the heart of feeling deeply, helps us to see.

The Mother as Creatress is the Lady of the Water, in the pure enjoyment of pleasure, bestower of gifts and wishes, healing the blood water. She is known to be psychic. She is clairvoyant lifting muddied muck-stuck places of personal conflict with change. This trans-fire energy creates mists in the water (mystic), that are used to help channel in-between-void, known as a gift, a blessing way, a birthing channel. Together relationship naturally forms to create life and aid all creative arts.

Move into your purest state of creation… mother, sister, daughter and grandma! Our birth rite is we bleed as water that creates and gives life. Even though men, sons, fathers and grandfathers are not genetically the birth canal of water, they heal and contain a great source of connection to this Healer Creator Mother. Those who are willing, ask and open. We will experience a great mirror of our likeness, of our Feminine power and Masculine healing through this medicine of listening and receiving, caring and tending. Soon we will discover these old barriers that were asked of men folk washing away by her waters of life, revealing a masculine softening that sends waves of rest and serene peace wielding a blend of visioning our servitude, enlightenment and devotional heart awakening.

I am breathing in and exhaling my worth. Receiving your words, each sentence hits a deep familiar place that I have protected and kept secret. I am safe to share and see others and speak from my own truth even as truth washes away instantly and sheds the parts of me that others might see as soft, feminine, kind and strong. I want those words for me, but they sing into me, into other realms, other pictures, places that are new with old faces. I'm new. I have changed even if my roots sparkle and are different. I'm feeling, although my heart is solid this time, it has cleansed me out with my consent. I am the Creatress of these heart songs of my own wellspring. I am no longer choosing to tend or care for others in the old ways that I have. I'm free. I am healed. I am what I am.

~ Jewelz

Move into your purest state of creation... mother,
sister, daughter and grandma!
Our birth rite is we bleed as water that creates and gives life.
Those who are willing, ask and open. We will
experience a great mirror of our likeness...

~ Jewelz Ann Lovejoy

In Her Intimacy – Initiations & Gifts

The initiation of the Creatress is to no longer fear caring for your tenderest places and most vulnerable parts, to place these foremost in your arms like a beloved babe being held by the Mother. The gift in this process is learning to love all and thy self, not separating from this inter-dynamic web of creation. The Mother as Creatress shows us without the vessel of our own being we would not be able to bring Her vast and wondrous works to life and each other. Her prayer is that you allow life to deeply saturate you with its rich multitude of pleasures.

May you drink in inspiration, allowing creation to bless and bestow Her breath upon it all. May your hands and voice, your limbs and organs, your body and sexual nature, your tears and laughter, be seen by you as the medium of expression of Her holiest love.

Dreaming

Dream with and as the Creatress... breathing Her alive through you. Doodle. Draw. Jot down your own wisdom from this intimate connection to the multi-faceted nature of your Feminine Soul.

Mother as Leader

The Mother as Leader moves by what stirs her, sharing songs and tears of grief, joy and confusion as her guidepost for how to live richly in love with it all.

© CATHERINE GEE

Passage

What is it you do not trust in yourself? The Mother as Leader will take you into your deepest distrust to uncover the undeniable wisdom of your own being. She stands with you before your essential nature – seeing the person you have always been and will always be. As Leader she walks you through the most dreaded and awe-striking terrain where you once slammed the door crying out, "but I don't know anything," "I'm not smart enough," "I have nothing to offer this world and no expertise." She shows you what you know beyond your own reason, holding your hand as you walk towards a steadfast resolution and deepening trust. The Leader grants you access to the pathways you deemed impassible by catching you when you stumble or try to run. She turns on the light when you forget you have your own. She shows you your choice points and crossroads, understanding that to truly offer guidance in this world will call forth our servitude to our inner soul and promptings.

To heed such inspiration means living in the flow of being you in each moment and with each breath. The Leader goes to the source of inspiration a million times a day. She is vulnerable to completely being unraveled so more wisdom and possibility may shine through. The Mother as Leader casts the arena of a new playing field. Gone are the ways of others instructing each other on the how-to's of life. The Leader within awakens our inner trust in Her, and knows that all we do derives purpose and sustenance from heeding our natural direction in sovereignty and interconnection. Separation from our Source becomes impossible, as the life of a babe in-utero grows not without the belly she is encased in, in the womb of her mother. In this way we learn what allowing Her love to enshroud us feels like. Her wisdom has little to do with showing us something we do not already know. Her wisdom is satiated in the unification of our being, knowing the more authentically and fully She moves through us, the more we experience our own nature.

Blessing

How could you ever believe you were not loved... you were not guided? I am the friend who never leaves your heart – reminding you life was created to forever sing you forth. The trees whisper their love for you. The birds sing of your joy and sweetness. The stones share your steady grace. The soil below your feet guides you to yourself. Every aspect of creation is an expression to guide you on. There is nowhere that sacred leadership is not. It is in the notion that you <u>need</u> to be led or that another needs to be taught, that true leadership is forgotten.

If you believe something doesn't already exist and feel it needs to be created, you've lost your greatest potential as a source of inspiration. If you call forth the resources within to discover where and how something is *already* in existence, and ask to be imbued with this wisdom, the ultimate leadership will be shared through you. Sacred sister, I am the one you can turn to when you feel lost and alone, when you are in doubt of your purpose. These moments awaken your true talents as Leader. These places of opening and releasing resistance to your inner self, help you discover the resources that are and will become your source of leadership for life. I do not exist outside of you, but awaken in your heart, body, soul and mind each time you feel you've gone off course. It is through surrender to this deeper knowing that you already carry within, that leadership is built upon, making you an open expression of love for others to witness creation unfold from. ~ *Mother as Leader*

Prayer

Sacred Wisdom ~ Holy Order

Show me how to lead from you as my beginning. Guide me towards my own renewal so I may look at all the ways I've feared unification with power, wisdom and love... with my own face as Leader. Bring me to the Mother. Help me release all former understandings of intellect, learning, instruction, guidance and education, so I might truly be open in my innocence to the grace of my soul. Help me see all the ways I've discredited the magic and mystery you've instilled in me, preferring to listen to what others say over my own resolve. Help me see all the doors I've closed to authentic guidance, confused that another, or you, could ever be separate from myself. In my deepest humility, help me turn towards you, into you. May my actions uplift all life so no aspect is seen or perceived as outside of your love. Great Leader, guide me towards these qualities in myself, so I may live most fully even with this fear of the message I am to reveal. Help me to live boldly even through my deepest fear of becoming the messenger I am made to be. Beloved Wisdom, guide me to honor all others in their inherent knowing, and to speak out when truth is not shining bright. May I be a Leader in divine grace, acting only for the true freedom of all creation. May no heart be crushed. May no spirit be downtrodden. Help me to not hold back even when I am afraid of the ways you show me how to stand in and up to my life, so all lives might know leadership as a journey back to ourselves, forever loved. Thank you. Amen.

Wisdom

To lead as a Mother means we cannot deny our soul stirrings. To lead from the wisdom inside our being means we cannot turn from feelings that awaken each time we experience life. The Leader is tracking her inner landscape at each turn,

© CATHERINE GEE

honoring this as a map to guide her direction. Like a pregnant mother who eats, sleeps and moves in unison with the growing life within, the woman who engages the Leader treats each of her moments with care and sacred inner listening. This becomes the foundation and way in which a woman as Leader shows up to love and ravish the world, and to be fully loved and ravished by it.

A mother who follows her inner Leader is humble to others looking for such an example, thus she holds nothing back. She brings her fullness and emptiness into each situation to offer all she can of her source harmony. How she lives in presence to what *is* present demonstrates a reality for all to be nourished by. No longer do we then place emphasis on sourcing truth from the out-side world. Turning inward to the Leader we demonstrate truth with each breath and step.

A woman as Leader defies long-standing structures, systems and institutions, coming into each moment and experience with faith that the most life sustaining system is the connection she holds to herself and her creativity. Leadership is showing up to this at each bend.

When you're in the presence of one who has tapped into her Mother as Leader, you notice she needs nothing from you, yet is willing to receive all you are and wish to offer. She knows there is no purpose but to move through life mutually, hand-in-hand, arm through arm, heart open to all hearts.

The Leader is the part within us that knows we have no purpose but to be together. Her wisdom is knowing that Leadership brings us closer to each other in holy reflection. Until we touch our own sense of being lost and confused, feeling like we have no purpose or direction, we will not open to the Leader inside. She comes to our aid when we're willing to cry out for someone to show us a way. She moves in like torrential rain revealing the resources we have within and around us to support our next steps. The Leader is our humility to acknowledge we are nothing without each other, and we are everything to all others. A Mother in her Leadership turns life on its heels and awakens us to the truth that we are the pathway and access point that brings it all together by grace.

Leadership is not an act of standing above or behind,
but reaching out from the greatest power and
vulnerability within to proclaim,
"How may I love thee more deeply?"

Engagement with the Leader

- Dance... dance some more.

- Allow movement to empty you of notions and guidance. Feel the presence of your breath, heartbeat, sweat, blood, pulsation, muscles and limbs. Invigorate your sense of how to move forward and take your next step.

- Caress your body. Say to your skin and cells, "You are the encasement of my Leadership. I am the Mother as Leader. I listen and follow you."

- Follow a child, creature or plant for a few hours. Breathe into this as sacred leadership.

- Ask your Shadow, inner fears and hardest edges to guide you for a day. Let this carry you into what is most real, true and tender about you and your life.

- Place a hand on your womb/belly before you speak. Draw wisdom from this cavern of your living leadership, grace and wisdom.

- Notice the ways you feel shy and afraid to be the leader of your own life. Perform a ritual. Embrace your smallest self.

- Learn an even deeper truth about your leadership through your tenderizing.

- Lead by doing nothing special at all... by being who you are without effort or false pretense.

- Create an artistic piece to express yourself as a Leader.

- Find out what you would do if you simply let yourself be.

Artist Insight & Offerings

I realize a path of learning also includes acknowledging, embracing and transforming those more challenging faces of myself.

~ CATHERINE, OUR LEADER

© CATHERINE GEE

The past four weeks for me has been intensely focused in the physical realm – paying attention to dis-ease and discomfort speaking from deep within the body as a path to connect into Soul. The gift of Listening Closely has been finding new doors into the realms of healing, light and love.

Bringing awareness to the voices of judgment, criticism, fear, and anger, the Leader within has been called upon to practice loving kindness, keep an open mind, and develop patience. Noticing there is a choice: to be open, willing to nurture and explore the essence of one's mind-body-spirit or spiral down in deconstructive patterns of ego and despair. Noticing a breath of fresh air occurs amidst adversity as the Creativity Muse waves her wand: colored markers, pencils, and paper appear from the back of the shelf.

There is an opportunity to express feelings, thoughts, sensations and be inspired by a sense of Play!

I continue to bring awareness and cultivate access to Light, Divine Wisdom and Love. I realize a path of learning also includes acknowledging, embracing and transforming those more challenging faces of myself. Tapping into sources of loving action towards Self, opening my heart, expressing truth and vulnerability in relationship with others are key ingredients to my own healing and transformation. I am also on a journey to discover, utilize and share my gifts and abilities. I aim to create sacred space, to cultivate soulful presence in relationship and interactions amongst others. I am learning to let go of expectations. Some days it can feel like I am in a very solitary place. Though I know, in continuing to connect to Source, I sense what is emerging from my very own Soul Essence. I am trusting that I Am exactly where I Am meant to Be. I am consciously creating and contributing in this world through my Life's expression.

The 13 Faces of the Mother sacred project provided a landscape and journey to explore one's creative potential and relationship to the Divine, Source of All That Is. Delving into the Face of Mother as Leader has been a most intimate exploration of Self and the Creative Process.

Mother as Leader brings forth opportunities to experience birthing, to express one's creative impulse of being and doing. Turning inward as Leader there emerges a continuous exploration of the depth and breadth of the vibrations of life, of both Light and Shadow.

The Face of Mother as Leader
listens closely, observing and facing
voices of judgment, resistance, fear,
hope, loving kindness, gratitude.
Mother as Leader
engages in a myriad of interactions, taking shape and space, leading, following life experience in form, transforming into soulful expressions.
A depth of feelings and insights emerge as visible and tangible creations.
An awesome experience of connectedness and play!
Leader within
Surrenders. Embodies Trust. In stillness, Listens closely within. Imagines and

expresses the creative impulse from within. Shares her unique expression with family, at work, with the World.

As I continue to face my fears, tears, and emotions that have heightened since the full moon, the words of Mother as Leader have been a key grounding and guiding force.

Blessings to divine passion, to the core of the Beloved, the sacred eternal fire, the source of creative passion, the creative LifeForce. It is here, there, everywhere: birthing, living, and recycling in you, me and we!

~ CATHERINE

In Her Intimacy – Initiations & Gifts

The initiation of the Leader is to live into the loud, ferocious, wild untamed nature of your wisdom, not to prove anything to those around you, but to show you what you are made of. May you trust that your leadership is inherently impactful beyond what you may ever realize or understand with your intellect. The Mother as Leader prays you play like a girl in the forest, permitting herself to pick up sticks, leaves and stones, moving on to whatever next captures your gaze. Her gift is to allow forth the knowing you are unstoppable and the world is waiting for what you will craft up next. The Leader's deepest prayer is that you never stop dancing.

Dreaming

Dream with and as the Leader... breathing Her alive through you. Doodle. Draw. Jot down your own wisdom from this intimate connection to the multi-faceted nature of your Feminine Soul.

Mother as Regenerator

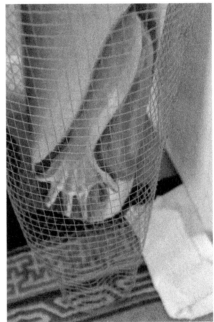

© CATHERINE DART

*The Regenerator is unafraid
to reach into the decay and
decomposition. It is here she brings
forth your glorious strength.*

Passage

When you begin to connect with the wisdom and power of the Mother as Regenerator, you'll go back through time to retrieve parts of yourself you've discarded, lost or deemed invaluable. She will bring to life the deepest gems of your being out of the ashes you proclaimed as castaways. The Regenerator calls forth what you've lost perspective of, incubating in Her reserves the treasures of your spirit and the wisdom of your womb, until all is ready to be reborn and shine. The Regenerator is unafraid to reach into the decay and decomposition. It is here She brings forth your unmatched strength. As we come into Her personal cycle of stasis, oftentimes we pull away – fearing we've grown old and withered, our gifts no longer useful. It is in these seasons of our heart's passage that the Regenerator is at work – devoting Her care and expertise to our resurrection and renewal. To truly be of service we allow the cycles of our lives to naturally come to pass. Our own stasis, incubation and resurrection are closely linked. Through Her regeneration, we release attachment and resistance to our outer form and that of this world. Our bodies, relationships, ideas and notions transform. We become the beings we've longed to be. Working with the wisdom of the Regenerator offers a power unmatched by this world. This is the grace of a caterpillar that knows it was designed for something more, and out of that knowing instinctively builds a cocoon for its regeneration. Here it will die to itself and be reborn into more of who it is.

Blessing

Dearest Child, I hold you in your smallest state and in your greatest expression. The two conditions are never separate under my gaze. You begin somewhere, and that is everything. You grow into something, and that too, carries it all. Come to me when you feel depleted, withered, washed out and away. These are beckoning signals that I am waiting for you. I've built a chrysalis and it is now ready for your rest. Let me weave it around you, wrapping you close and safe, bound from and woven into time, space and your earthly responsibilities and existence. In this cocoon you are kept warm. I nourish and care for you. Can you trust me and my purpose for your life? This may feel like death. You may resist or long to run, not seeing the blessings of my gifts. Yet you are not designed to go on forever as you are. You are not designed to always move as you do or believe only in your current perspective. You are designed to change and transform... to walk, run, scamper, flit, fly and be free. My cocoon is a sacred chamber for your resurrection. A space to review your life and open to the parts you've tossed away. Your original nature is what I weave around you. Breathe it in as it imbues and supports the creation of your next form. Breathe it in until you can no longer claim you are anything but all that you are. The journey to me may feel fearsome and confusing. It may go against everything you've been taught about your own success and the reality of this world. Yet the first touch of my hand's craft, the first grace of my wisdom, will change all you've believed about yourself and what is possible. You've believed you have this one life to become all you can be. And somehow you fear you've failed! Let me show you that within every moment the existence of 10,000 breaths lives. Let me wrap you in my stillness and assurance to feel the ever-changing truth of love's present journey. Discover freedom. It is your choice. ~ *Mother as Regenerator*

Prayer

Beloved Seed ~ Great Chrysalis

Take me into your cocoon of Regeneration. Holy spirit – humble love, restore me to my deepest sustenance made of your fiber, sweat and tears. From the beginnings of time you've loved me. May I clearly look at any and all ways I've blinded myself from your care. Till the end of time you reach for me – calling me in to the chamber of my resurrection. May I clearly look at the ways I've turned back, running from my own transformation. Show me my fears – every one of them. Show me my grace – every aspect of it. Show me how to give up and slow down and curl into you to be restored by your vision of me and what is possible. Take me to the arms of the Mother. May Her regenerative power reveal who I truly am. May my masks fall away. May my heartache become unstoppable. May I call out to Her with ferocity, knowing I am designed to emerge from this cocoon and be reborn. May my journey be an example for all others, how to walk this earth in your humility, power and grace. I long to serve the regeneration of all life. May it be done through me. Thank you. Amen.

Wisdom

We are born into nourishment and live by life's ceaseless giving of sustenance. We grow into being givers and nurturers as we allow the rhythm and timing of our own regeneration to unfold.

Through regeneration, a woman brings to life and embodiment the full brilliance of what was a tiny seed within her. Each step of the way, this seed has imbued her life and choices with distinction. As we allow our deepest regeneration forth, this seed matures, blossoms, dies back and regenerates to distill into more of the purity we are, into more of the purpose we are here to sow and share.

The barren landscape of winter beautifully depicts the process of natural regeneration. We cannot see what is occurring. To our eye it looks as if all has died around us. Yet so much is happening below the surface, in our souls and interconnection, in roots of plants and the soil of our earth. We can use the eyes of our heart to trust and feel what is occurring deep inside when no outside activity reveals. This is the initiation and gift of the Mother as Regenerator.

And this is one of the hardest things for someone to access in our modern culture and fast-paced society. Much emphasis has been placed on what we can see, on productivity that is visible, countable and accountable. Yet it requires the absorption, rebuilding and regeneration that can only occur during these wombing times for us to unfold and move into the flourishing of our true productivity. Little value is placed on the deep, underground, fly-below-the-radar cycles of our creativity. Here we learn to trust ourselves. Here we come to understand what contributes to well-being.

A woman who engages with the wisdom of the Regenerator learns the art of self-trust through all that will come. The cocoon of regeneration helps her turn inward to the depths of herself and her inherent creation. She learns to trust the entropy and involution, the descent into the darkness and being held here until timing is right and sunlight returns. As a woman awakens to the Regenerator within, she gains a new relationship to timing and rhythm, and with her unfolding natural order.

The power of the Mother as Regenerator is symbolized in our cycles of incubation in the pregnant womb. To the actual mothers, we can turn to learn this deep wisdom. Our mothers and the Mother within us all, knows how much is happening inside our bellies, inside our bodies and the folds of our being, even when we can't see or touch it. This is a sacred and significant part of our lives. During these first months in utero, a fetus grows and transforms more than at any other time. Here lies great wisdom.

When we as a culture honor the cycles of apparent stasis and regeneration, we begin to see beauty in a new light. We honor our elders and cherish the pacing of infants. We don't rush the natural order, touching it within the recesses of our being to draw forth ways of seeing life with a fresh perspective through the vast freedom of one who has just developed wings.

A woman who engages with the wisdom of the Regenerator
learns the art of self-trust through all that will come.

Engagement with the Regenerator

- Watch the stages of a butterfly or other regenerative creature (i.e. ladybug, spiders, etc.).

- Get or build butterfly and insect houses. Order larvae online. Communicate with these creatures. Witness their growth. Set our regenerative wisdom free.

- Curl into fetal position. Wrap yourself in blankets like a cocoon. Listen to the sounds of water, waterfalls, whales and dolphins. Restore.

- Create a piece of artwork/expression that is from your time in the womb/in utero. Allow whatever wishes to come forth to unfold.

- Journal about resurrection.

- Harvest seeds in autumn and dry them throughout the winter. Plant them in the spring.

- Say to yourself, "I am a Mother. I am the Regenerator." Breathe.

- Tune into the Regenerator before falling asleep. Talk with Her like a child, praying for all areas of your life you wish to be renewed, reformed and regenerated. What is possible?

Artist Insight & Offerings

I saw it as a chrysalis.
And from this chrysalis, it also became a womb,
for is it not, in truth, one and the same?

~ CATHERINE, OUR REGENERATOR

This has been a very present and meditative process. I have been coming to it again and again, being very open to all possibilities, and trying not to put anything preconceived in my mind into play. It is most interesting and I am thrilled by it. At present, I have the stirrings of a couple of ideas and their directions and am letting it continue it's swirling inside me. Deep, pretty much in my pelvis.

   This piece was a revelation to me. It came slowly at first, and yet once I caught its scent, I saw it as a chrysalis. And from this chrysalis, it also became a womb, for is it not, in truth, one and the same? And as I worked with the materials, sculpting its form, I again was struck by the very immediacy of the connection between the chrysalis and the emergence of said butterfly, or baby: a doorway! And this opening, from one stage to the next, is also known as the vagina. What an amazing synchronicity for me to discover. Of course! It's all there for us to see now, but I had never made that connection before. In that sense, it was a real gift of dialogue and trust.

~ CATHERINE

I feel like the other artists are in a similar space in this journey as we unmask ourselves / ideas. We shift with our hope and fear. It's from here we will spin what it is that needs to become for this project.

~ Catherine Dart

In Her Intimacy – Initiations & Gifts

The initiation through the Regenerator is for the deepest vision and longing you hold in your soul to arise like the butterfly emerging from the cocoon... in her most perfect time and natural way. Her gift is your own unshakable trust coming forth, in birthing your deepest self and its natural order. The Regenerator helps you feel a sense of exhilaration, knowing everything you've done in your life has led to this. Nothing is wasted. Nothing of your past experience is worthless when viewed through Her Womb's creation.

Dreaming

Dream with and as the Regenerator... breathing Her alive through you. Doodle. Draw. Jot down your own wisdom from this intimate connection to the multi-faceted nature of your Feminine Soul.

Mother as Priestess

© DANA GILEM KLAEBE

*The Priestess has no need to interpret
the workings of your soul.
Her purpose is to be with you in it,
and to show you what
you are made of.*

Passage

The Mother as Priestess is your guide into the great mystery of your being. She is here not to help you solve riddles, or to be the translator of ancient texts. She arises within you to reflect the immensity of your sacred existence beyond comprehension. The Priestess has no need to interpret the workings of your soul. Her purpose is to be with you *in* it, and to show you what you are made of. It is here you will discover what is possible of your life, not through intellectual understanding but through a deep primordial experience of your being. When you long to know more of who you are, it is the Priestess you are calling upon. She spans the edges of your self-comprehension and lovingly carries you into terrain beyond what your mind can endure. In Her landscape, butterflies soar over molten lava and dragons lay down at your feet offering unworldly treasures. Her realm is not solely of mythic legend. Hers is the power of creation that lives not by constraint. Our fear of the Mother as Priestess within us exemplifies our modern-day confinement in a landscape that is two-dimensional. The Priestess' wisdom takes us into realms where we call forth our own healing and gifts, not through outside sources, but through the deep authentic connection with all that is possible in mutual creativity. The Priestess asks us to be outlandishly innocent, outrageously wild, vigilantly mature and in highest integrity to our sacred self. This is not about losing connection with our practical nature or the deeper reserves of our intellect or analysis. This is about harnessing it all and seeing where such unification can take us.

Blessing

I bow to you sacred Priestess, for I know in this realm we are mirrors of each other and there is nothing I can give you which you do not already contain. We are the holy reflection of true wisdom, seeing in one another what is true within ourselves. Come to me, vulnerable and ready, open and transparent. Fear not your own fear. I look into your eyes and together we breathe through any scorching resistance, accepting who I know you are. You are the brilliance of creation; your body's contours reflect every detail of my mystery. Know yourself deeply. Touch your womb, your heart and blood. They each carry the wisdom of life – offering the ground of humanity's homecoming. Look in the mirror and see my temple. Notice the fire glowing in your own eyes. Feel the stirrings of your passion and know it as significant and your true life's work. This is what trans-forms our communities into kingdoms, into the holy lands they are intended to be. Place your hand upon your heart and feel my alliance. Together we face eons of forgetting that within you rises the wisdom of all ages. This is a solitary pilgrimage. One you will take into the wilds of yourself. Sisters will support you spirit-to-spirit. Family and community will gather around, connecting heart-to-heart. I am with you in a form that is eternal. Amidst this a moment will come when you'll be asked if you're willing to proceed forth on your own. Your authentic answer is pivotal and cannot be made wrong. This passage can feel like grave solitude. You are crossing a threshold into your own sacred sovereignty. No one can claim such terrain but the conviction of your own soul. And here you will find everyone standing, encircling you as a witness. Never again will you feel confused about who you are or where you belong. Lay down the fight Priestess. You were born to shine amongst us. ~ *Mother as Priestess*

Prayer

Dearest Sanctity of my Soul ~ Holiest Temple of my Being

I tremble, afraid to claim the power that lives within me. I long to know myself in the Mother Priestess. I shy away, fearing harm will be done to my humanity. Walk by my side each step of the way. Hold my hand in the moments I feel most alone. Help me enter the forest at midnight. May I recognize the wild terrain as friend. Great face of the Priestess, bring alive the Mystery through me. Help me share its stories to liberate all from our own static convictions. In your eyes I remain true to my spirit. Help me strengthen my own reserves so I may be true to Her always, carrying such purposeful grace and wisdom inside my being to be offered in a fleeting moment, for the awakening of all. In the darkness may we turn to you – allowing our fear to reveal what is real.

In my innocence may I accept the beauty of the Mystery that I cannot tame or unravel, even from within me. Help me delight in the awe and wonder. I am the Mystery. Knowing this is more than enough. Thank you. Amen.

Wisdom

There is an awakening happening in our current culture as the feminine is remembered and women reclaim the instinctual wisdom of their own being, lineage and

ancestry. The modern day Priestess is arising! This is a homecoming of a woman unto herself. It is the harkening call of our culture, for all men, women, children and community, to celebrate the sacred ways of our ancestors, intuition, natural rhythms and holy ordinary rituals, of our deepest connection as brothers and sisters, and true kin.

For centuries, the realm of the Priestess lay hidden beneath shrouds of veil and cloth, covered under a mystery that set such wisdom apart from the everyday workings of human life. And with good reason. The life of the Priestess went against doctrine of religion and patriarchy, of family structures and cultural institutions, of time and space itself, and all that attempted to lead from the outside, proclaiming wisdom as separate from nature and each other. Within the rituals of the Priestess lived the wisdom of abiding connection with creation, of an inherent resonance between humans and plants, creatures and kin. The Priestess awakened through her direct relationship with life and source by listening to the inner guidance of her body and sexuality, of her instincts, visions and dreams.

A woman who opens herself to the wisdom of the Priestess oes through a subtle and obvious transformation. She learns to harness her sovereignty and to intrinsically connect with creation. She is able to allow a deep intimacy with life's rhythms to guide her. This is on a profoundly practical realm, one in which the workings of life are revealed through direct daily experience. The wisdom of the Priestess does not take her away from the world and her relationships, but brings her closer to them, holding a remembrance of how sacred we are to each other. In this she knows how important it is to live in service to creation and its intrinsic flow of beauty, breath and truth.

As women reclaim the energy of the Priestess, there's been a natural distortion of Her wisdom as cultural dogmas and expectations attempt to fit Her into pre-existing conditions and limits, into an overly masculine model of spirit and ancestral traditions. The Priestess does not and cannot live here. She lives in the wilds of our hearts and the forests of our wombs and vision. To work with Her is to grow intimate with one's own insanity and clarity. The Priestess is the power that takes you to the edge of all you've known and trusted, beckoning you through primordial landscapes to reclaim direct connection with your people, land, creativity and the cosmological forces. As you trust this process through your own synergy, you learn nothing can guide you forth. The ways in which you will find your way and formulate reality come from the places within that no one but you can reach and draw out. Here you'll find 10,000 companions to lead you on, through thresholds you'll ask yourself to rise and pass through. Here you become a human reaching with everything you have for the sacred and the divine.

To work with the Priestess can feel like walking in different realities at the same time. This is Her pathway. Its purpose is not to have you choose one as more valid or important than the other, but to support you in keeping one foot in each dimension, in your heart *and* in your head, in your womb *and* in your soul, in your imagination *and* in your practicality. By doing so, a Priestess becomes and shares all she is through all she does. This blesses the pathways we can and will tread as a people and community, opening doorways into new possibility and into the reality where all we do and share is sacred.

As a mother allows herself to be a Priestess, she returns our basic and mundane reality into the divine truth that it is for. She provides a foundation for all to know themselves as creations of the sacred. A mother has the power to reveal the deeper wisdom of our passages, activities and transitions as seen through the vision of our ancestry and royalty. The wisdom of the Priestess turns homes into castles, children into royal descendents, dysfunctional relations into holy family, and all of life into the dynasty of our soul. Caring for children becomes a high order. Preparing food is seen as the healing alchemy it is. The Priestess offers her unique touch of love into challenges and hardships turning daily life into an ongoing ceremony. Following one's inherent sense of ritual and rhythm becomes the spiritual communion we all long to know and share in together.

Entering the order of the Priestess is as commonplace and acceptable as the daily life endeavors we engage in. It brings our intuitions and wisdom to the foreground to bless and be blessed by all. This is a journey of sacred realization and true self-initiation. As a woman surrenders to knowing herself in the wildest places of her mind, heart and source, she will deeply craft her life from the reality and mystery of the Priestess within.

I AM the Mystery. Knowing this is more than enough.

Engagement with the Priestess

- Awaken your full nature... of your heart, mind, body, soul and convictions. Notice inner places you keep separate from. Allow, welcome and breathe into the spaces where love is collaborative.

- Trust your intuition. Trust it even more.

- Place a hand on your womb/belly. Refer to your inner being with all decision making.

- Notice the distinction between 'going it alone' (connecting only with your mind), and asking for your inner Priestess (your womb/belly region) to support and guide you.

- Craft, create and form your own ceremonies and ritual for family, community and personal milestones and transitions. Trust what comes forth.

- Listen to the moon. Open to the sun. Feel your relationship and intimacy with the planets. Ask your inner Priestess what is most vital for you to know and heed.

- Enter the wilds of your soul. Go on a Priestess Retrieval. Plan a few hours/day/weekend to commune with Her. Connect with nature, make art, dance, follow your instincts, journal, listen, be in silence. What is it you cannot deny about yourself any longer?

- Say within your heart, "I am a Mother. I am the Priestess."

- Create an artistic expression with and of your Priestess.

- Talk with the animals. Notice which types, breeds and kinds you are drawn to *and* afraid of.

- Become like an animal and notice what you'd like to do, eat and have.

Artist Insight & Offerings

She hears the wood and water
and embraces them with all of her self.
The moon pulls on her, shaping and making,
opening eyes to truths
both ancient and new found.

~ Dana, our Priestess

Generally, my process for creating a work of art involves reading and research on the subject. After I've moved through the research portion of my process, intuition begins to take over. I let my feelings and instinct guide my process... which colors will be dominant? How will I connect the viewer to the work itself? Ultimately, the creation itself, especially with works like the Reindeer Priestess, take on their own life force and engage the viewer.

As I've moved through my deepest feelings of self, ancestors and wildness of the forest, my inner priestess communes with all creatures and beings that are seen or at times hidden from our loud and sometimes chaotic lives.

Part of my creation process and really, my daily life process, is to read. I'm drawn to my ancestors and the worlds and lives they kept sacred. It brings me great joy to connect with others feeling the pull of the ancestors. :) I feel blessed to have been able to hear them as a young person and to have had parents that didn't try to turn me away from my path.

~ Dana

She was always meant to live with you.

*The idea of creating a work and sending her out into the world to
inspire and bemuse others... well, that makes me happy. And I know
that I've been true, to myself, my ancestors and the great mother.*

*There is such joy in my heart because I know her. She
is me. I am her. I love being a woman!*

~ Dana Gillem Klaebe

In Her Intimacy - Initiations & Gifts

The initiation of the Priestess brings confidence and forward movement of
sharing the innate gifts you have as a Feminine Life Artist through many forms
and ways. The Priestess helps you navigate thresholds of wild landscapes where
nature and modern life intercept and collide in your heart, where soul and practicality dance and merge, knowing balance and grace through you. The gift of
the Priestess is to rest amongst the trees, feeling your deep organic sense of
place and home, and allowance of your creativity running as the wise one. Her
blessing goes forth with you upon stampeding horse's legs carrying her wisdom
and gifts, knowing that her message, call and sharing is needed at this time,
exactly in this way. The prayer of the Priestess is to call yourself homeward,
always, in Her name.

Dreaming

Dream with and as the Priestess... breathing Her alive through you. Doodle. Draw. Jot down your own wisdom from this intimate connection to the multi-faceted nature of your Feminine Soul.

❧ Mother as Bestower

The Bestower deeply lives in the principle that to truly come home to oneself is to become a welcoming home for all.

© CONNIE PETERS GULICK

Passage

In the ancient folds of your being you will find Her face – our Mother as Bestower. She affords a rare glimpse of your deepest nature in primordial perfection. She provides you with sacred serenity... a solace to truly see yourself in your most simplified state. Not as an aspect that has had nonessentials stripped away, but as the deepest essence of your being before, and alongside, all that has piled up to shade the grace of you shining. The Mother's bestowal does not come from outside your form. It awakens – strong, steady and serene – to rise within, offering moment-by-moment reconciliation with the intricacies of your incomprehensible creation. Her power is a wellspring offering cleansing water to the weariest of travelers, affording satisfying nourishment for one who has spent lifetimes seeking. To spend time in Her wisdom is to accept yourself in the state of your own wholeness. She is the honor that returns you to the fulfillment of your being. Ideas of selfishness are as far from Her reality as you have been from your greatness. The Bestower deeply lives in the principle that to truly come home to oneself is to become a welcoming home for all. As we live into Her all-encompassing presence, we are awakened in our core. We become the center of love for creation. As you sit with the Mother as Bestower, allowing Her to caress your folds and share in the ways your presence in essence is enough, you'll be providing this ultimate bestowal to others. To be with Her is to live in the darkness of your inner chamber and no longer search for the light. To partner with Her is to feel contented with needing no guidance or direction from outside. To journey with Her is to rest in the all-enveloping blackness and feel your way through undiscovered intuition – to feel the inner texture of your soul, womb and holiest knowing. This is the language of the Bestower – the template of Her expression. She becomes the anchoring proclamation cascading with love's deepest message, "You are enough as you are. Feel how this never ends."

Blessing

Honorable Daughter, loving yourself can never be underestimated in its impact on all of creation. Being with me is discovering this naturally within. You were created as a formation of the Divine. Every intricacy of your body, brain and spirit were patterned upon perfection. Every nuance of your thinking, being, your breath and heartbeat were resurrected out of ultimate love for all existence. You cannot spend enough time saturated in this wisdom. It is *this* knowing that will awaken my power within so never again will you devalue the beauty of life and the totality of being. Each time I look at you, through every facet and phase of your journey, I see perfection discovering more of itself. You've perceived yourself as injured, violated, broken apart and ripped open. You've seen yourself as less than, greater than, worthy and unworthy, needing something you do not have. My precious, receive my wisdom and feel your completion. Feel how you could never be any of these things separated, on their own, without everything else. Allow yourself to sit with who you are... this is who we are together. My presence bestows the deepest remembrance in you. You begin to feel the grace of all life pulsing and no longer are drawn to pursue what takes you away from love, and from complete rebirth. Some may hear these words and see them as selfish. Some may be afraid that to choose to live with me means to think only of themselves. This is as far from my reality as possible. The more space you create to live into your preciousness, the more you serve the deepest beauty of life. Words and explanation fall short from conveying the wisdom of my path. To Bestow means to offer blessing to all of creation ALWAYS. To allow me to ripen inside you, forming you as the Bestower of life, creates an intimacy between us where no longer will you do *anything* solely for your own purpose. Open your being and receive my wisdom, love and grace. Out of this intimacy, you provide a rich reserve for others. Never again will you question how may you serve. Your breath, gaze and touch, this expression, are my bestowal. This flow carries forth unimpeded to serve love. Allow it forth daughter. ~ *Mother as Bestower*

Prayer

Divine Grace ~ Sacred Mother

How may I live in the bestowal of your grace? How may I become the deepest resource for all life? Place me in the hands of the Mother as Bestower. Take me to the power of Her deepest creation – the power that formed me as I am, beyond my own comfort and comprehension. Help me feel the majesty of my being – the wonder of my thoughts, moments and living experience. I do this so that I may come alive to and with your love. I do this so I may share this everywhere without ceasing. Help me venture into the landscape of my human existence, so I may be steadfast in proclaiming the sacred value of creation at every turn. Holy Wonder, bestow on me the richness of a heart broken wide open to your grace so the love I feel may pour without end. May everything I touch come alive by you. May everything I say awaken truth in all. May everything I bring attention to reveal unmasked beauty for all to behold. I long for my life to be the ultimate bestowal of divine experience. Bring me as deep into my humanity as I can go to touch the lives of all with the incomprehensible presence of the Mother. I move towards you now and always. Cling to me like a lioness holding her cub. Place me down where I can grow into the regal power of servitude and bestowal for life. Thank you. Amen.

Wisdom

The Bestower offers an opening to the range of creative expression that lives in our soul and through what we are here to share. Photographer, scribe, collector, poet, collage artist, painter! The Bestower comes out of nowhere. She is the raw magic that's been hidden from our own eyes. Poof! A wand reveals to transform all things to truth. Things on the surface are never what they seem... look what's been resting within you and in our world for all time?

The Mother as Bestower initiates us into endless and ordinary treasures. To see them requires an innocent gaze that only one who has lived a life such as yours has the power to see, draw forth and reveal. This is the passage a woman will walk when she opens to the wisdom of the Bestower. She'll discover her life and body overflowing with rich gifts and reserves of creation. Even through despair and anxiety, she'll see the rain as a reflection of the Mother's tears alongside her own. The Bestower is akin to a fairy godmother, yet not in the traditional sense of taking us out of our current reality to a "better" one. She arrives and ingrains into our hearts, revealing the princess living in the pauper... showing there is a Queen even when we see a slave.

Like many of the Mother Faces, the Bestower opens a pathway through our being that can feel terrifying and exhilarating. We're walking into a domain we've never quite allowed ourselves to enter before, yet have intimately felt, known and longed for with all we are.

A woman can hold herself back from the wisdom of the Bestower because it crosses the boundary of her greatest vision and intermingles with her deepest shadow and darkest wounding. Suddenly what is dark is light. Things are not what they appear to be on the surface. Poverty becomes the greatest richness. Isolation awakens as the deepest intimacy. The reality of this world takes root in something penetrating and unshakable found within our natural existence.

Within the Bestower's grace lives a truth we are endlessly blessed by – being who we are. The wounded feminine feels frightened about 'giving too much' and being taken advantage of. When she first encounters the reality of the Bestower, she deepens into this pathway within, knowing it is through her own revelation and validation in intimacy with creation that the real bestowal will unfold.

To walk through our daily lives and be amazed by what exists around, below, above and through us is the wisdom and grace of the Bestower. This cannot be forced or manipulated. With the Bestower as our guide, this becomes a sublime and natural occurrence; one we never saw coming, yet knew all along was real and here.

The Bestower within is the safekeeping of our sincerest dreams coming alive to reveal the poverty of our hearts and deprivation of our souls for what they are... our own negligence and denial of the richness that lays dormant and accessible through our creativity of being. The Bestower unites us with our longings and shows us they are fulfilled under our own feet and through our own hands.

You are enough as you are. Feel how this never ends.

Engagement with the Bestower

- Go for a walk. Slow down and breathe.

- Notice the Bestower everywhere.

- Keep a record of Her face and blessings. Pick up Her mementos.

- Spend a day giving... giving to you, nature, another, life, through whatever form feels uplifting.

- Invite friends and family for a celebration of giving and bestowal. Feel what wishes to take shape. Have people exchange appreciation, witness beauty within, and share special mementos with each other.

- Experiment replacing notions and language of "you" and "me," and "I" and "thee". See yourself in all others and they in you.

- For every instance in which you are drawn to give to another, give to yourself. In every instance you are drawn to give to yourself, give to another. Play with the wisdom of the Bestower who sees no separation between us and our giving-receiving.

- Create an artistic expression of the Bestower. Express what She offers, how She sustains, and how She nurtures.

- Say within your heart, "I am a Mother. I am the Bestower." Breathe and feel.

- Write a letter from the Bestower to you. Allow the heart wisdom of the Bestower to express all that is treasured, honored and appreciated about your being and this one rich life.

Artist Insight & Offerings

The Bestower will not be contained.
Her wisdom keeps recreating itself
and what is bestowed will multiply.
It must be given again and again and again.

~ Connie, our Bestower

I am astounded. I am stunned. The face of the Mother, Bestower, has taken a turn towards photography. I have been photographing "Bestower" for many moons. I can't stop taking pictures and picking things up off the ground. Her gifts are all around me and I can't take my eyes off them. It's nearly all I want to do. I must listen. I must gaze as she gazes upon me ~ through every little thing I encounter, even in my own mess. The gifts are endless as I am open to receive. I know deeply that I have been blessed beyond understanding. This photo study is but a small sampling. The Bestower will not be contained. Her wisdom keeps recreating itself and what is bestowed will multiply.

It must be given again and again and again.

It is what lives in us, through us, for us. It is what is seen all around us and only in part.

Be amazed.

The eyes of the Mother are our own and she wants us to see. Of course she does.

It is recognition that is bestowed. It is love of the deepest kind.

That which cares about what is careless, seemingly small and messy.

My wonder ~ my joy. It is yours. It is an endless circle, the cycles of life.

It is what it means to be human. To be alive.

To be rock, plant, flower, animal. Elements, water. Sun, moon and stars.

It is what we all breathe and how we fill our time.

It is time and beyond time.

We are small and we are insignificant in isolation but each piece of our own creation sings to the others. Each leaf, each drop, each flower, has something to say.

We sing together of the Bestower as we continue to give our gifts.

Each tree, each mess, each growing opportunity.

Made up of many parts, it is myriad. So many pieces that while beautiful alone, create the whole. It is what we are. It is where we live.

It is what the Bestower wants us to see.

Behold.

Receive.

Continue to give.

I took over 2000 pictures this year. After spending countless hours going through them and selecting prints, I've had quite an assortment to work with and choose for our project. I was feeling sure which ones were my favorite. Thinking this would be an easy task while my parents were over, I put them on the table before they arrived.

My mom went right over, wanting to rearrange them, telling me how they should go together. She had the idea they should be grouped by color. Before we left for dinner, she couldn't stand it and went back to the table to show me her idea. She laid some of them out in new patterns and I said, "Yeah, yeah." I had the attitude that I will still do my own thing.

Later, I looked again at her layouts, then packed the photos back up to the studio, determined to follow my own course. When the time came to prepare the prints to share with everyone, I realized I had way too many. My own developing ideas needed to be pared down. Hmmmm.

Faces of the Mother intersected with my own mother. She had an inspired contribution that helped solve my dilemma to narrow the field. I decided to frame the combinations that I "worked" on with my mom and hung them in the house to honor her."

The eyes of the Mother are our own and she wants us to see. Of course she does.

It is recognition that is bestowed. It is love of the deepest kind.

~ CONNIE AQUILA

In Her Intimacy: Initiations & Gifts

The Mother as Bestower enfolds you as you reclaim the treasures of your being at every turn. The magic of your wondering, the open nature to yourself in its priceless value, is Her passionate gift and commitment to us all. May each day be a clearing and cleaning so you can see what has lived within for all time. May you come to know yourself through the eyes of the unicorn, and ride upon his back to the refreshing waters of this beauty you have carried for eternity.

I must gaze as she gazes upon me ~ through every
little thing I encounter, even in my own mess.

~ CONNIE PETERS GULICK

Dreaming

Dream with and as the Bestower... breathing Her alive through you. Doodle. Draw. Jot down your own wisdom from this intimate connection to the multi-faceted nature of your Feminine Soul.

Mother as Beloved

The Beloved will not play the game of duality.
She will not enter the field where
contrast or comparison is applied.

© CONNIE PETERS GULICK

Passage

To feel so cherished that you live in love with self, other and life at each turn is the grace and power of the Mother as Beloved. She is the entrance to your own reality where all creation is interwoven in love's sacred design. The Beloved sees Herself not as apart from any of it. In that way She beckons life closer – to and through Her – wanting to explore, create and greet it all. The Beloved feels held by and intricately woven into the exquisite balance of love's existence. Her wisdom stands tall, gentle, strong and serene right at center, welcoming all eyes on Her with devotion. Knowing with certainty that what others see in Her is what *they* truly are. And in kind, She offers the same, till each gesture of heart's gifting is a seamless ripple between every living thing mirroring life's only truth. We are the Beloved, every particle, every crumb. Often we perceive it can only be our 'perfect' package of self that'll be adequate enough to express the gifts of the Beloved. Yet the Mother smiles upon it all. Every aspect She holds in Her hands calling out, "Oh, this is so precious, this is so essential, and this is so rich!" She proclaims this even to the hardest edges of our own journey. In this power one can only stand in the grace of oneself and accept who we are, as we are. The Beloved will not play the game of duality. She will not enter the field where contrast or comparison is applied. In Her deepest truth She knows all life is gracefully interwoven, and She has no need to pull things apart. She knows beyond reason that the whole and sum of its parts are one and divine.

Blessing

Beloved, oh my dearest Beloved, to look at you brings endless tears to my eyes. To see you in form, growing, breathing, living, is a dream realized. My purpose feels fulfilled to know that you are. I cannot express what your life means to me. It is the feeling of a Mother looking into her newborn's eyes for the first time, every time... stroking his skin, feeling her beating heart as my very own. This is how it feels as you open and welcome my power and wisdom within. I see you as a living angel, beyond all time, being birthed into this world each moment to serve as you are. I wish to share this feeling with you always. It takes child-like wonder to know this, yet also a significant maturity and depth of life experience to allow it forth. Every moment is the creation of the Beloved. Every person, every place, everywhere you turn and touch brings this reality into aliveness. Let me pour my delight for you upon you, so you may share the same with all others. It may feel a bit over the top to some, or like far too much, this level of sacred realization. Yet every time a new mother looks at her babe she weeps, seeing only a miracle. That is what my wisdom is as it awakens through you and through all. It does not shy from the challenges or ignore the deep valleys of suffering. Far from it. It travels with you there so you may grieve even more deeply for the truth of how much you've loved and been loved. This cannot be bound. My heart of the Beloved can be heard wailing across continents each time an aspect of itself is hurt, injured, desecrated or passed on. Not because I cannot

live without it, but because I know how precious it is and was to live *with* it. In my reflection you will never again be able to hold love back – within yourself or with all others. Your heart's passion shall pour forth like sacred blood bleeding from a broken open heart. You are my Beloved, and so is every aspect of creation.
~ *Mother as Beloved*

Prayer

Sacred Mother ~ Holy Living Father

Take me into your arms so I may see and know myself as you see and know me. Help me clear away years of false perception that I've placed upon my life. Restore me to my sacred innocence. I wish to return to the purity as your Beloved. I long to know my face as the expression of your love. I long to feel my heart in its enflamed pulsation of life's deepest truth. I have suffered, believing my humanity, my body, work and choices did not live up to all that they could be. Did not live up to the divine example. Bring me to my own divine revelation so I may fall in love with who I am and have always been. Send me endless opportunities to discover sacred ground in the passage of my days. Remain by my side when I discredit my healing, my own beauty, wealth and movement towards my soul. May I cherish my existence as the Beloved's living form and expression. And as I discover a deepening joy in being me, may this extend beyond what I imagined my life effects, to convey love to all. We are the Beloved, all of us, embracing ourselves ever more deeply. May I turn to my sisters and brothers, welcoming this rich care into our interactions and life history. Our lives are far too precious not to see what is true forevermore. Thank you. Amen.

Wisdom

To speak of the Beloved can seem like a trite romance. Yet it is far from frilled pages of a story of bedazzled lovers finding fulfillment through each other. The path of the Mother as Beloved is heart wrenching. It tears apart everything you've

© CONNIE PETERS GULICK

believed about love, God and creation, until you're empty and naked, feeling like a newborn babe helpless without the other. Helpless without the Mother. This is the condition in which the Beloved within will be found and restored. This is the space where the love you've been seeking from an outer world transforms into an all-consuming longing to be ravished and remade by the Beloved within.

This is the place where the Mother will embrace and care for you. You may choose to claw your way into and through this tunnel of transformation. You may rest in Her arms in surrender. Your fullest rebirth can only satisfy your insatiable hunger. No longer will anything from the outer world feed you. It is She inside that will show you the pathway home.

Many will feel this is a drastic expression, proclaiming there is no need for suffering or struggle. This is accurate. The Beloved has no interest in creating our suffering. She wishes to undo all pain and strife, so we may find our way through it and enter the chambers of our distortion to discover who we are and are created to be. Through this inexpressible quest we find an end to suffering, and can thus aid the world in a life without struggle where we open to our deepest pain. In the Beloved's embrace we find love's freedom, cradling us in our own arms as we hold and tend the heart of the world.

A mother enters the journey of greeting the Beloved each time she moves with the birth of a baby, vision or new possibility for her family and/or the planet. The Mother as Beloved walks with a woman every step of the way upon this path. We cannot birth without being birthed. We cannot create without becoming creation. There can be no love offered without being the love that offers. Entering any form of Mothering becomes our pivotal passage to the Beloved we seek. This is like the moment we look into our child's eyes and see ourselves as God sees us. This is a pinnacle experience when we allow ourselves to passionately share our gifts with the world and accept the transformation and healing that is brought to others, to heal our own selves. The sacred tapestries we weave and are inherently woven into are the great work of the Beloved's hands. There is nowhere Her heart is not. It is stitched into the seamless fibers of our interconnection, into our living experience of family.

A woman beckons the Beloved forth, yet she'll have to ask herself how dedicated she is to the journey and its enduring course. To know the Mother as Beloved in oneself is to claim the glory of becoming not only who you are but also who we can be, together, unified through our distinction.

To caress our own skin and imagine what the Mother must feel as she connects with her living creation is an act of service to all of life. When we come into the presence of our Beloved nature within, we never again take life for granted, most especially our own existence.

The woman who enters this domain reveals through her presence tenderness and vulnerability for this path of uniting with the Beloved. It is apparent through her gestures, in her eyes, through the way she talks and words she uses. Yet no one form or fashion will convey the ways of the Beloved. It is revealed through every form and face that has chosen to lay its life on the line to find, intimize and know love without question. This may sound like a far-fetched, unrealistic commitment. Yet this level of relationship to our inner sourcing and sacred reality is not for the faint of heart. This takes determination and commitment. It takes vulnerable actions and an innocent willingness to show up again and again. And not in the way we've imagined or society has proclaimed... in the way of the natural order, like the trees and plants we witness around us, or the creatures whose lives are lived through primal instinct. This is the pathway of the Mother as Beloved that lives to benefit all without end. She is found by discovering our unending desire to know her within our own hearts and all of our relations.

My heart of the Beloved can be heard wailing across continents
each time an aspect of itself is hurt, injured, desecrated or
passed on. Not because I cannot live without it, but because
I know how precious it is and was to live with it.

Engagement with the Beloved

- Sit. Feel. Breathe. Sit. Feel. Breathe.

- Laugh, cry, get up. Sit back down. Follow the flow of your being through the Beloved's adoration.

- Go for a treasure hunt, retrieving gifts and symbols of the Beloved. Spread out the items and take in this reflection.

- Share your love. Give your heart and soul through your work, parenting, daily life, vision and creativity, your sexual encounters, eating and cooking. Offer the fully ignited flame of the Beloved within.

- Grieve wide, vast and full for things, people, creatures and situations you've lost.

- Accept yourself. Accept another.

- Volunteer for something that inspires you.

- Caress your body, feel your skin, move with the rhythm of being adored.

- Say something you've never said or feared sharing.

- Create an artistic piece to express yourself as the Beloved.

- Say within your heart, "I am a Mother. I am the Beloved." Feel this.

- Take an action you've never imagined you would or could.

- Hug someone you were afraid to or felt standoffish with.

- Forgive unabashedly, including yourself. Be willing to disappear.

- Look in the mirror and see yourself through the eyes of the Beloved.

- Carry the fullness of your heart in your own hands each day.

Artist Insight & Offerings

You are born of desire ~
We return to desire. It is that simple.

~ CONNIE, OUR BELOVED

I AM
Beloved
I
Conceived
You

I AM
Wisdom

I have created you ~ I continue to create through you.
You are born of desire ~ My desire.
Our desire.
We return to desire.
It is that simple

Rest in me ~ I have full knowledge of you
    Restore in me
        Be healed in me

Find what you do not yet know you desire.
Your truest desire
Seek

IT IS HERE

I
AM
PEACE

~ Be at peace with me
~ Let me hold you here
~ Wherever you find yourself today

We are One
We are born of desire.
We are birthed to be together.

Such a needed time, this season, for beginning to balance my own energies in some new ways. I recently had the privilege of fulfilling a long time dream ~ to study at a monastery in the Bay area. I arrived there incredibly tired and in need of some real regrouping. During introductions, I told my class I was in need of some rest and wanted to sit with the Mother. Soon after, I discovered it is not called a monastery when there are women. I was actually inside the Motherhouse of the Sisters of Mercy. At one point, we were given a ball of clay with our eyes closed to have a new experience of it. I was able to keep that going when I realized it felt like the coolness and weight of a baby's hand or foot. I spent a good while napping with it, understanding more deeply that it was actually my hand that was being held.

A few days later I bumped into a Native American man with a drum. Knowing there was no time limit or expectation, I boldly asked for a song. He happily went right into an incredible chant, familiar but not. At first the only word I could recognize was family. As I continued to listen, he sang of the Mother. And how we are one... and remembering. He showed me some of his woven cedar artwork and described the eagle feather as a symbol of balance and fidelity. In relationship and fidelity to oneself. To our gifts and bringing them to the world. Eagle Bear carries a drum to remember where he comes from. To be reminded of his mother's womb, where he could hear her heartbeat and her voice. He told me that his father passed away and that he now sings his father's songs to keep them alive. I have two of his cedar roses to add to my paintings. I am very full now. May it spill over with grace.

~ Connie

At first the only word I could recognize was family. As I continued to listen, he sang of the Mother. And how we are one... and remembering.

~ Connie Peters Gulick

In Her Intimacy – Initiations & Gifts

The initiation of the Mother as Beloved is like the waters we ceaselessly thirst for. When we take our first sip, the Beloved's gifts permanently restore and fulfill us. Her face is the one that turns over in our minds, blessing us with unbeknownst discovery of ourselves. The Beloved's gift is to give yourself richly into your rebirth, allowing Her to walk with you, to whisper to you, to truly gestate within as a Mother until you are ready to be born, no sooner, no later, indeed in perfect time. May the words you share, the expressions you offer, the gifts you carry within, reflect the ancient wisdom of your source and the connection you've forged here as Her Beloved, never to be forgotten.

Dreaming

Dream with and as the Beloved... breathing Her alive through you. Doodle. Draw. Jot down your own wisdom from this intimate connection to the multi-faceted nature of your Feminine Soul.

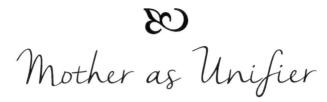

Mother as Unifier

Share your artistry here! Express, intimize and
be innocent with the Mother as Unifier.

Throughout this journey, each week I sat with and lived into the Faces of the Mother, holding each woman close who was working with that Face's expression. A prayer would come forth, a passage, Her voice offering a message. I'd share this via email with that particular artist the next week.

For the Unifier, everything was different. The message was clear. Now each Feminine Life Artist (myself included), was entering this passage completely, falling in love and trusting herself to rewrite each component of her life, reality and story from her own connection, conviction and expression, from her deepest intimacy with creation. Our *Faces of the Mother* journey ends in the Unifier. Yet it is the beginning for each woman and for us all, to delve into this passage in ever-lasting sovereignty – in authentic permission to see our whole being and life as the Unifier's living example.

This is my offering and prayer. May you trust yourself as the Unified Mother. May you follow what is alive and well from inside, all the way into completion and expression.

We all long to feel and see what you know...

Passage

To know the Mother in Her unified state we live into Her, breathe through Her, allow Her to rebirth our being from Her own blood, breath and bones. We become Her, harnessing unboundable love through our own hearts, bodies, minds, selves and souls. Our lives become the awakened truth that proclaims every aspect of creation *is* Her living devotion. And every aspect of ourselves is an expression of the same. We are the unity, knowing that within and through us lives a reality that cannot be translated, refined, downsized, torn open or labeled. It is far beyond and intensely a part of it all, inseparable. To truly engage Her wisdom, we allow every aspect of who we are to be redesigned from the pure originality we were created from and in. We surrender to every Face of Her taking form in and through us so we might experience the deepest humility and power that strives for nothing, but chooses to love and serve *everything* from our living humanity in each moment. In so doing, we are cradled in Her grace and no longer need search for self-definition. The power of the Mother in Unification cannot be spoken of, only danced with through our life's passion, until one feels a doorway within her own self open into everlasting intimacy with Her. Never again will we look to know anything from outside of our own being.

We will talk about the things the Mother is not, but we can only directly live into and experience the wisdom that She is. When we choose to no longer hold back, to no longer judge ourselves or confine what we love to tight corners and restricted areas of our being, She begins to guide the way. When we fall to the ground weeping, feeling as if we cannot take another step forth, She becomes the Source from which we take our next breath. When we no longer rely on outside definitions or opinions, standards or expectations, She begins to show us life's deepest rhythms. When we've forgotten how much we matter, and don't believe our life has any purpose, She holds us as she did when we were a babe, proclaiming, "My child, there is nothing within you that I do not love. We are inseparable. You are everything to me. Without you I would not exist."

The Mother as Unifier is expressed moment-by-moment through all that we are and will do. We cannot turn back once we've reached Her... only move forth, tenderly rewriting this journey from direct knowing of all we shall discover and forever be.

As you look through the expressions in our *Faces of the Mother* Collection, you come to see that for each form to awaken and be created, the Feminine Life Artist discovered the Mother's living Unity in herself. Through each woman's own connection and experience of this Unification each face was formed. And so it is with you...

As you awaken to the unending force of the Mother within, you live your life through Her deepest care, adoration and guidance, merging evermore into a unification that has no bounds – between you and I, between She and We, between this and that, between us all. As we each touch this incomprehensible power within, we become the living unity of Her grace and grow evermore assured that who we are, as we are, is a revelation.

Blessing

Write your message from the Mother as Unifier...

Prayer

Write your prayer and deepest longing to connect with and become the Mother as Unifier...

Wisdom

Write your wisdom through connecting with and becoming the Mother as Unifier... for the well-being of all humanity.

Engagement with the Unifier

- Breathe. Inhale. Be. Let in You.

- Exhale. Let go. Allow. Share who you are as you are.

- Create, and create some more. Never stop.

- Value your creations. Celebrate your manifestations and your decompositions.

- Share ways you are and have engaged with the Unifier – send us your stories, poems, pictures, artwork, realizations. Connect us all through you!

Artist Insight & Offerings

I AM
Basking in the gifts of Bestower
Being with Beloved
Experiencing the Unifier

What if?

What if our real work is not yet done?
What if there is so much more?
What if Unifier wants to rise up in our midst?

To create yet again as we come together...
To produce something new...
A visual representation not yet conceived...
Perhaps something else...
We are held by the Holy Mother.

I pray with you and to you dear Sisters. That we shall remain open.
That we shall sensitively listen.
That we will hold space for each other. For Sharon. For the Faces of
the Mother Collection.
To see this work through to completion.
To open wide the doors to the rest of our work.
That which is still to come forth.

This is big, Sisters!

Do you feel it?

~ MUCH LOVE FROM CONNIE WHO IS NOW ALSO AQUILA

And now CREATE an art piece or sacred expression of the Mother as Unifier. Share it with us... share it with the world. Your self-judgment is not necessary. Together we are co-creating our *Faces of the Mother* Collection.

Send your creative works to sharonannrose3@gmail.com. Let us see and validate how we all weave in Unification!

In Her Intimacy – Initiations & Gifts

The potency of this process comes alive through us all. As stated, this book is a backdrop. Its words, visuals, expressions and journey offer a way, and many ways, to celebrate what is possible as we listen to our longings.

YOU are the living cover of our *Faces of the Mother* story... the ever-changing expression of its wisdom and grace. The initiation that occurs through this passage can only be directly experienced, spoken of and shared through each of us. The gifts of the Mother are made real through our works, breath and inherent nature as Feminine Life Artists. This is not for a select, trained or elite few. This is inclusive of all – from those in the farthest reaches of civilization to those in the mainstream, educated or not.

Encompassing our fullest lives and validating everything within, is the REAL deal... the true expression of the Mother. And this is touched and initiated through us individually in our deepest innocence. May it fully come alive as we come together in our love for life.

The Mother as Unifier is and always will be within us. She lives as we vulnerably acknowledge and celebrate we are designed from one body and breath, from one heart and impulse of love.

Live as if your voice matters. Live as if being who you are can, is and will change the world for the betterment of all. Love your living, no matter its face and form. It's the most sacred gift and rich resource we've got.

Let you be you...

There is no end to such beauty.

An Eternal Passage... letting in you

It's a painful process
and you have to wait
you have no control
and when you get done
you start all over again
from scratch with someone new
who is coming again from a place of nothing
to a place of knowing
And you feel like letting go
And you feel like letting go
And you feel like letting go
so you let you be you
and discover things you never knew you had
find strength inside you didn't know you had

~ ANNA SODERBERG

Dreaming

Dream with and as the Unifier... breathing Her alive through you. Doodle. Draw.
Jot down your own wisdom from this intimate connection to the multi-faceted
nature of your Feminine Soul.

PART THREE

A FEMININE RESTORATION

Gathering

We came together, eleven women in honor of the thirteen Mother Faces we'd opened our souls to, to engage the expression of our creative lives. We looked upon a seascape of sisters, revealing our vulnerabilities, meeting in the flesh for the first time. We peered at a tapestry of mirror-like expression, seeing our dreams, fears, deepest shame and holy existence reflected through each woman's work and sharing. We spoke boldly and timidly whispered. We felt light and talkative. We laughed and grew silent, deepening into ancient space with a new, yet familiar title for ourselves, "Feminine Life Artists."

I emotionally held this moment to my breast, learning to call out with humility and power for its ensuing implications. Eleven women bared witness to something awakening, restored in coming together as we were, soulfully naked in this imperative value of our Sacred Feminine restoration.

A month after our *Faces of the Mother* journey completed, we came together face-to-face as women and artists, as creators of our feminine restoration. Eleven women joined in circle, one engaging from Canada through the Internet. We sat, many meeting for the first time, and lit candles, exposing creative truths and awkward experiences. We shared our Mother Faces through a tender humility that so often in our culture is seen as weak. Through such softness we bestowed stories and trials, knowing *that* was why we had come. Here we knew we would be safe. Darkness and light had revealed itself upon our passage. Now we offered its full face in thanksgiving.

I felt nervous, excited, relieved and in awe, seeing the physicality of what had been worked on in the interior realms of our hearts and lives over the past three months. *Faces of the Mother* was birthing right before me and through us all.

I sat amongst these women, familiar now as kindred, and looked at each one's face and sacred artistry. I felt a tangible sensation course through my body. This book, these creative works, and all that would ensue, was being formed in this moment by us coming together. It's a feeling that's never left and is what allowed me to drop in to my feminine wisdom throughout this process. In that moment I drank in the depth of its message. It helped me validate and continue with this body of expression even when I wanted to curl into a familiar mindset, proclaiming I had nothing of value to share. I'd remember the faces of my sisters and the sensation that pulsed through. In that moment I knew I was not, nor ever could be, in this alone. *Faces of the Mother* was not solely for me. This became my anchoring breath and touchstone.

We began our gathering in the weave of co-creators, bringing together strands of yarn, ancient gifts, stories and wisdom from our ancestors and journeys, creating a symbolic and energetic loom for this collection to take shape. My offering was the raw manuscript from this book's introduction as our backdrop and entryway.

While reading my words aloud I felt myself tremble; my face grew hot. I knew in this moment and in each to come, we were letting go of debilitating patterns, shame and perspectives that proclaimed us as anything but who we truly are – Feminine Life Artists, co-creators of the sacred. I sensed I'd never turn back and sent a blessing to all women as I imagined this tipping point occurring in the collective. Within our circle we contained the far-reaching presence that shifts a single moment into the eternal. The power of being witnessed in our deepest gifts has an everlasting impact.

What poured through me in the weeks leading to our meeting had been drawn from all we'd experienced on our three month pilgrimage. We ended our journey just after the autumn equinox. On that threshold, I fully committed to outlining and bottling some of this freshly touched substance up from our collaboration.

It was a clear transition to make, moving from holding the container of our shared journey, to entering it fully for myself as a personal creative process. One morning as I sat down at the computer to write, the energy that had been gestating came rushing through like the waters of life after a placenta breaks. Labor had begun. As I paused to take a breath, the whole first part of our book was before me in form.

From the inception, our Feminine Life Artists shared a deep yearning to meet their fellow artists. The question arose during an early part in our journey,

"Would we?" With certainty I knew we would, though sensed it'd be orchestrated through our creative collaboration, versus any singular efforts I'd be coordinating. I didn't offer parameters, nor have a sense of structure for how it would come together. In my belly I knew it'd occur in the most impactful way. I trusted. Each woman held a similar energy. Yes, we'd meet one day and look into each other's eyes.

With little effort every one of us was able to join together on a late autumn morning in November at my creative womb sanctuary. Housed in an old Masonic Temple, our gathering brimmed with the intensity of our feminine hearts. It was a simple coming together of women, sisters and kindred companions. Each Life Artist lit a candle to honor her Mother Face and shared what she felt inspired to from her journey, process and of her artistic expression. Some shared about the actual process and what had unfolded. Others offered more about the form their creative expression took. Each woman was held by our rapt attention. We knew what it took for her to stand before us, revealing this tender bit of her soul and feminine landscape. And in equal measure much occurred in what we did not say alongside what was spoken. We wove our sister from Canada into our gathering, moving an iPad around to rest before each woman as she shared her story, offering a snapshot of her Mother Face.

At the center of our circle stood thirteen glowing candles. Twelve rainbow hues forming the perimeter around one pure white one. As each candle was lit and that woman spoke, it was palpable something was lit amongst us. We felt how the Mother and inner landscape of the feminine was being born. We embraced a spectrum of possibility beyond what we could comprehend or attempt to express. Here all was cherished. Within and amongst us the sacred work and reality of the feminine was restored.

Our coming together revealed the many faces of love's reality. Through every one of us this is authentically made known. We all have color. We each hold a part. We offer a significant and creative way for life's passage. We each ignite a passionate fire none other can. As we stand side by side in this ignition, we demonstrate something not of this world. Yet it is through us that this truth becomes real. It's what we mutually long and live for, to intimately know and experience love through our every day lives and form. And through our willingness to hold each other's hands, we discover it is real.

In our gathering each woman accepted the gift of who she is, sharing it amongst us to bless all. In circle we welcomed, received and called forth each woman's soulful expression, discovering this as imperative for a culture, community, family, government, business and social system to thrive. This is the authentic journey of our feminine reclamation.

We closed with a song sung by Sarah, our Mother as Distiller. The lyrics are included in honor of our journey, listening to and revealing the heart songs of our feminine restoration.

Listen Closely
by Steven Walters[1]

There is a song only the heart can hear
Listen closely
Older than time, yet fresh as the fragrance of a flower
Is this melody

Poets and lovers
Have spoken of the song
Such sweet despair
Reach for this and
It's closer than your hand
Let go and it's there

Then the music
Such sweet music
Suddenly the music is everywhere

Sing the mountain
Sing the rising sun
Sing the flowing river
In the valley just beyond
The mystery has no ending
It just goes on and on

Sing until the singer is the song
Gate gate para gate para sam gate bodhi swa ha[2]

---

1   Steven Walters, "Listen Closely" from the CD, 'So Many Blessings' http://stevenwaltersmusic.com/

2   "Beyond the beyond"

Friend I know
That you can hear this song
I see the melody in your eyes
I needn't know your name
The song it is the same

May you always hear this music
May your heart be filled music
May all hearts hear this music
And our voices fill the skies

Sing the mountain
Sing the rising sun
Sing the flowing river
In the valley just beyond
The mystery has no ending
It just goes on and on
Sing until the singer is the song

There is a song only the heart can hear
Listen closely
Gate gate para gate para sam gate bodhi swa ha[1]

---

1 "Beyond the beyond"

Feminine Restoration... a path of Co-Creation

*It feels especially good to dedicate and apply
myself to something so meaningful.
Every woman should be as fortunate to realize that each
offering is sacred and that we are "enough" as we are.
This kind of Grace opens us to so much more and I
see myself right in the midst of that dynamic.*

~ CONNIE, OUR BESTOWER & BELOVED

Co-creation is an art and lifestyle choice. It takes practice and commitment. To live in honor of all we do through its mutual implications, comes from a shared field of our inherent inspiration. This takes time to meld, restore and reveal. The first realization begins in the recesses of our being. In the folds and tissue of our flesh and sovereign experience. We are always creating with the divine.

I've been searching my whole life to truly know, acquaint and intimize with my source. I recall a passionate longing since childhood to know God like a best friend, and spent much time as a youngster in the natural world, talking to the spirit I found living and breathing through nature, plants and animals. One day, more recent than not, I realized what I longed for most was to touch the source of the natural divine within myself and body. This longing, though not overt or recognized, drove me to go deeper, to lift the corner of any covering I could find, and to push those closest to me to an edge. I wanted to see the organic face of the sacred through every aspect of my existence, even my physical form.

This was the impetus that our *Faces of the Mother* journey grew from. Yet until I ripened, settling in to joyous responsibility for this as a personal mission, I could not realize the pathway here or through. Through this rising passion I would learn to touch and follow the source of the sacred within me. I would discover how to create my existence by accessing this sovereign place that is a sensual and innocent love affair with the origination of creation. This is how I began to tenderly touch the power and possibility of co-creation.

Here I faced the everlasting choice that to rebuild my life I could choose to accept and delight in the reality that I never walk alone. I am always capable of calling upon the creative to inspire my work. From this I can form and share what my soul inherently knows long before any words or clarity will be spoken.

Faces of the Mother became a living testament to the process of co-creation. It offered me a rhythmic and practical practice for how to commit to my wellspring of inner source intimacy while holding a place for others to sacredly create out of this resonance.

Each step of the way our circle turned to the Mother to exemplify love's reality. To Her we wept as persistent notions of separation rose to the surface. As inner voices shouted, "You have to know what you're doing to begin!" we asked Her to show us another way. And when we believed we had to follow an outer defined structure, we prayed to Her to reveal our inner sourced path. On and on the journey went into facing our greatest shame and devaluation of the wisdom of our feminine way. Each woman claimed a passage and initiation into the sanctuary of her soul's fertility. Here it was inevitable we would come face-to-face with the expression of ourselves and the Mother as one.

It is to this personal and collective partnership with the full feminine force we drew upon to reorient us to the truth that we are in this together, creating life and our dreams from a shared field of longing, mutual existence and sacred humanity. *Faces of the Mother* is an expression of what is possible as we rest in the arms of a divine personal embrace, while seamlessly weaving and being woven into the workings of others. This is co-creation.

Here we dedicate ourselves to remembering who we are, what we are made of and what we long to express and share. This is life's real blessing. And this is how we find our way home. The ideas and stream of thought that awoke through the writing of this book comes from us all. Creation itself imbued the 13 Faces we relied upon to guide our creative platform. The artwork and expressions of our Artists were forged from the fire of each woman's dance with source as she pulled in, stretched out, exhaled, inhaled, retracted, surrendered and opened to all she could contain and let go of.

Our lives are the living reality of co-creation. We never walk alone and are invited to open these doorways to our ancestors, to one another and the future of our planet… to the possibilities that lie dormant and ignited inside the folds of our flesh. Life is an artistry in which we're asked and asking to be who we are. May we share ourselves nobly for the well-being of the world.

I am happy, filled with grand joy. My insides sit here in blessed humor of our creativity and weaving inspiration, for as it is now ever changing and transforming its face. To capture the essence of your wisdom and others is superbly exquisite.

~ JEWELZ, OUR ARTIST & CREATRESS

Pause After the Journey

I had sensed it was coming, yet was blindsided as it hit. I was ready to dive in to the writing and weaving of these snippets and experiences of our *Faces of the Mother* journey. It was winter. I'd waited a lifetime for this. I was to become the writer I longed to be.

I asked the Life Artists to have all finalized pieces to me (their art work, descriptions and photos) by winter solstice. I envisioned a cozy inward season, mugs of tea at my side, clacking on computer keys in the early hours before daybreak. When I first became a mother I developed a ritual of waking around 4:00 am to meditate, pray, write and rejuvenate. This rhythm carried me through transitions in my mothering and family life. I imagined it would be the sound structure through which I would safeguard and actualize my intention to bring this book to life.

Whenever we set an intention, our daily life reflects areas and ways in which we're *not* yet fully committed to its actualization. Our lived reality shows us any adjustments that will naturally be made to bring us into our fullness. This is a universal protective measure for our own mercy. If we see it from the deeper intention it is offered through, we gain clarity about what bars such forward movement. We learn to breathe into the question, "What am I being asked to love within myself and life with everything I've got?" We open to our resistance instead of pulling back and completely away from our longing and endeavors. We grow through our inner source of sustenance.

As I engaged my longing to bring this book to fruition, every person (and animal!) in my family became sick. We cycled through illness many times over and experienced a winter like never before. In the wee hours when I envisioned I'd be writing, I was holding our youngest or submerged in a steaming bath to loosen my own congestion. There were few and then fewer moments to come up for air. I could only self-inquire on the surface into this experience before moving to the next family member's needs and my own health's tending.

During this time I remembered the power of the Mother and asked Her to show me a deeper truth about sustenance and creativity. I wanted to know what is possible in the darkest hour of my soul. That winter was about basic survival, and along the way I discovered an ultimate faith. I invested in prayer knowing 'this too shall pass,' and remembered a conviction that surpassed reliance upon the duality of external/internal methods of finding my center (ex. meditation, ritual, walking in nature, self care and inquiry). I opened to the chaos and trusted that through *this* She would be found. That winter I was shown I could *never* leave my core ground. Any such notion was a lie. I chose to remember and embody eternal home.

What I discovered is a flow that is always present. Through whatever comes we can open and engage our lives fully. Any fears that we will give too much or not enough, become drained or never get back to our centered selves, begin to slip away as we trust the cycles of our experience and ourselves within them.

We are always in harmony at our core with the greater expanse of our creative well-being. And this is not to say that meditation, ritual, self-care and inquiry, all the things we do to feel centered (like my precious walks in the forest) do not benefit our lives, creativity, health and connections. These become the joy and result of touching in to our creative core nature, and realizing what brings us true human pleasure. We each have a natural resting ground and expressive resonance. By tuning in to this we learn the basic ingredients for our soulful livelihood. We trust our implementation and expression of this to flow from our well-nourished lives.

Engaging here we will find a rhythmic balance occurring in our wholeness as we deepen into trusting how we hold what is appearing in our lives and through us as it is. We see what is before and within us without past wounding and judgment. This restores a deep-seated faith and inner wisdom that trusts the universal force of creation within.

Our giving and tending to life, self and others is not something we can orchestrate or balance within the chambers of our intellect or well thought-out notions. This is an act of love from our inherent soul fertility. As life creates, we are its sacred engagement. This is not the result of having to deal with something thrown at or out from us to harm. This is the result of being the center and original pulse point for creation, a living start-up button. Our outer and inner life is not separate. We are the expression of a far-reaching power and capability that continuously crafts and welcomes creative energy from the deepest recesses within. This fosters inner stability and our capacity to shine no matter how dark the storm.

That winter felt like being in a pressure cooker. I was often in tears describing to my husband this intense weight upon my chest. It was like having a perpetual heart attack. I felt like I couldn't breathe. Everything inside longed for the deepest presence of love that is possible for a body to hold. As my system reoriented to this prayer, I had a visceral and energetic heart opening. Through this I learned to be present to this pressure, discovering I could be where I was and still feel all that I am. With the Mother as base ground I allowed the wellspring of my feminine heart to reveal my true power.

I'd supported these ten Feminine Life Artists through their own creative unfolding. Now I was asking to show up to my own personal dreams, letting co-creation be more real than I'd ever been willing to admit. Here I embraced the darkness as a gift.

As She had said, "Learn to rest in the dark and no longer reach for the light." In the grace of the Mother's field there is no separation. The dark and light know each other in an intimate, whole, sensual and unified way. We get to simply be, and to know *that* is more than enough. This is the gift of life giving to itself all that it is. It is the joy of knowing that each of our experiences is beautiful, worthy, a blessing and gift.

That winter I saw how much of my life had been spent keeping everyone 'comfortable.' It is a natural tendency many women have and an important one for humanity's restoration. Yet when this is not held in the awareness of collaboration with the discomfort and darkness, it cannot serve in the authentic way it is meant to. By going through the *Faces of the Mother* process, my role and way dramatically shifted. Something in me let go. I would now live with Her one step at a time and no longer judge any of it.

As one of the Artist's stated in the aftermath of her process, "I think the biggest kicker for me is that when you keep giving – no matter what – you get the biggest 'reward'". I am so grateful I was held by the *Faces of the Mother* project while all that was going on. I felt so often like I was getting huge challenges... and each one felt like a little jab, or sometimes a kick. And then I was being asked, "Can you be loving and kind?" (jab, jab), "Can you *still* be loving and kind?"

Heart & Womb Creations

I held the Mother's hand today
It came
In the form
Of a ball of clay

I felt the Mother's touch today
Loving
Careful
Deliberate
Gentle
Questioning
Open
Providing relaxation
Studied
Unafraid
Nurturing presence
Hugging
Teaching me...

That
She
Is
Me

~ CONNIE

Something powerful occurs when a woman invests in and engages her womb and heart while flowing and forging through the process of her creations. Our womb is the space where we intimately touch all that has not been touched by this world. Here we open to our sovereign intimacy with what is sacred before it comes into being. Our heart is the space we live through our fire and passion; here we melt into the tenderness and care for life and others. As these energetic and literal storehouses of our personal sustenance and guiding wisdom join in our awareness, our creations come alive with a conviction, yielding and commitment to serve humanity. We are instilled with the blessings of our womb and heart. Creation is sustained through us and all that is to come.

I've carried a natural propensity to create with and through my heart. Yet it's never quite what it seems to be on the surface. Though I was aware of the womb, and the ways and power of working with it, due to my upbringing, past experience and natural proclivities, by default I seated myself inside the folds of my heart. My offerings to clients, my community, family and relations were filled with love and tenderness, overflowing with nurturance and imbued with an ability to merge without boundaries. Yet a pattern developed in which I did not feel sustained by my outer world or open to receive its support. I felt as if I had to exert extra personal effort to sustain life.

Without the inherent partnering with my womb, the creations of my heart arose on embers of a wild fire, turning to ash after the heat had died down. From the heart's chamber on its own, I was not able to sustain life's sacred warmth. I wasn't experiencing my precious existence as a sovereign being within my own form.

Through my work with women and the life initiations I've experienced, I learned to engage the wisdom of my womb. This is where the power and strength of the feminine resides. As I entered the womb space and worked from its cauldron, I wanted to offer my creations into and through my heart. I did not need to send, control or direct them here. Through our hearts our unique way of loving is kindled and fed.

The creations initiated in my womb were endurable. Their inspiration felt like a steadfast mountain, yet soft and yielding like a flowing stream. My relationship to sustainability shifted as I partnered my awareness with both my womb and heart. My womb allowed me to touch the sanctuary within my body where I lived with my creator and sourced creation. My heart allowed me to touch the oneness of life, where I lived within love's breath for all of humanity.

Faces of the Mother is my celebration and gift of sharing this unified place of the heart-womb within my being. Here I was blessed to support others in accessing and living from this within their own lives and creativity.

May we each welcome these opportunities to feel and share the deepest wisdom of our heart-womb sanctuary.

Heart-Womb Homecoming

The feminine literally houses herself in the womb. It is the sanctuary in which she comes to know herself against all odds.

For those who've lived more from their womb, a common experience can be a pattern of creating and living into the interior domains of life to such a deep sense of satisfaction, that you don't turn to the outer world in mutual collaboration and service. In the womb we forge our boundaries. And it is through human partnership that we learn how to soften them. Through the womb's wisdom we learn to work with our sovereignty, but may not access our natural ability to grow through partnership, community and oneness into the realizations of our heart's vulnerability and sharing.

The womb is the portal to our ancestry, lineage and past. It is where we learn who we are and what we are made of. Here we go to understand we are the origination and breadth of creation coming alive. Our heart is the portal to our community, sense of family and future. It is where we learn who we are becoming and what we are designed to share. Here we go to feel the landscape of humanity coming alive through our tenderness and passion.

The terrain of our body is designed in collaboration. Our organs and energetic chambers form a natural and inherent order. Our heart is the bridge for all above and below, bringing realms of earth and heaven together. It is the container for our connection, showing us how to meld and merge with life. Here we experience ourselves emanating into and blessing/being blessed by all of existence. Through the heart we come to understand time in an evolving, boundary-less, unified way.

Our belly and womb is the region of our personal connection and power to the universe and with the origination of being. Through it we learn to master our creative fertility for the well-being of existence. This is the bridge of the inner and outer, bringing realms of our inherent masculine and feminine into union. In the womb is where we experience ourselves plunging to the depths of timeless existence before it was. We come to understand our eternal nature through the internal journey of the womb into our living soul. Our belly and womb is the storehouse of our wholeness. We learn to be who we are as we reside here. And through our hearts we share the gifts of this full presence with all of life.

It is natural to be drawn to one area over the other because of past experience and our childhood environments. Interconnection within family, relationships, communities and culture, inherently pulls us into certain proclivities to create balance for the whole of existence. This is something we can learn to trust. It is a humbling awareness to see we are designed to be in service to each other. These times call us to know ourselves through all we are in our sovereignty so we can clearly make our way upon our path for the well-being of each other.

Our patterns of living from the heart or womb provide a natural initiation into the deeper caverns of our being. Here we learn to trust our source, ourselves and all of creation. These internal powerhouses support our dreams coming to life. Like our inner masculine and feminine nature, our womb and heart are designed to live in harmony. As we open space to trust this inherent design, we come into centered awareness, creating from inside our wombs and bellies.

May we gift these tender petals of vision to our internal fires to be ignited by the union of love.

Heart of the Womb ~ Womb of the Heart

On the surface nothing is ever what it seems. As we travel into this inherent collaboration between our womb and heart, we delve into terrain beyond distinction to discover the heart of the womb and womb of the heart. Here anything perceived as a wound or limitation becomes a pathway to something richer, wiser and enduring within. The inner chambers of the heart and womb reveal a face and side to ourselves we sensed, yet couldn't quite accept that we contained. Here we can find out how to make our way to the other side.

Our challenging life patterns and conditions become the restorative chamber for healing our heartache, grievances and pain. We open to the deepest nature of ourselves and the ever-spiraling, cyclical experience of life as we touch the core of the heart and womb inside the other. We are the living, breathing interconnection of existence, revealing how all things live inside all else. An acorn drops from a tree, and is what the tree grows from. Within an egg lives the embryo of new life, and the egg contains the possibility of new life that one day will be birthed from a mother's body to begin the cycle again.

Deep in the caverns of the heart and womb lives the other, anchoring these partnerships in inseparable existence and function. In my workshops I share a guided journey into this domain to discover what the heart of one's womb feels like. Allowing this to be tangible and brought into our awareness opens an unlimited core beyond the center of our womb space. This is how the hearth of the feminine grows alive to its inherent and unique glow, revealing the enduring fire of our being.

As a woman becomes intimate with and then creates from this internal heart-womb co-existence, a platform for her deepest wisdom is resurrected. She sees, will make real and validate the wisdom that is not logical but is nonetheless true. In this dance of her heart and womb, the feminine discovers her eternal voice and face.

Growing intimate to the womb of the heart opens a pathway for source connection to flourish through what we care most about. This feeds the embers of our passion and is how our love becomes enduring. When a woman opens to the womb of her heart she finds a maturity that is unshakable. She will face anything for what she loves. And though she will intimately know fear, she will also move forth in partnership *with* it, to continue forth in her deepest tenderness against all odds.

Finding the womb in the heart and heart in the womb provides insight into the distinction and interwoven relationship of life. Touching this within us becomes a direct source of inspiration and power for how creation works. This helps us grow aware of how we are all distinct and working co-creatively together, and our visions, dreams, longings and ideas literally exist inside other aspects of life. When we see the world through the heart of the womb and womb of the heart, we come to know all is inter-dynamically supported. We never create in separation.

Anchoring into these territories opens new doorways for *how to create*. This shakes up everything that has grown static in one's life and prior ways of going about things. Here we see that our creative capacities are ever changing and will be enduring. They continue to refine and grow more distinct as the pathways of the heart and womb into the other reveals our natural integrity. We experience a revelation that we are far richer beings, more unlimited than we ever imagined! We can continue to allow the lifeblood of our creative capacities to grow and flourish. Touching the womb of the heart and heart of the womb, reveals how every unique creative expression leads us to the next, and is a living dynamic that will draw us into and out from the sustaining network of our inseparable relationship to life inside of us all.

Intrinsic Value... a creative pathway

As we discover and cherish the value we hold within simply because we are, mountains move around and within us. Areas of our life we believed we had to work tirelessly to uphold or conform to, suddenly take on a spectrum of variable hew.

The artistic expressions of the Life Artists in our collection reveal the range of creative resources we carry and can use to demonstrate what we are made of. When we see we all have intrinsic value, no longer do we attempt to hide our fullness from the whole. The imperative to share our gifts because they belong to the greater well-being of humanity, prompts us forward.

The wholeness within us becomes a sacred platform where we engage with the source of our lives, bringing our worth and value forth. This demonstrates how much we care, about ourselves, each other, and every aspect of creation. Honoring intrinsic value becomes a pathway of connection to the wholeness of life. It is within us that the source of existence lives. And through us this existence is made known.

As we allow the fullness of our being to come forth and fuel our range of expression, we give permission to others to shine through the vast array of all we contain. We are more than we can make known through any one moment, person or experience. And through each moment, person and experience we foster the opportunity to glimpse all that lives within and beyond.

May we touch and experience the depth of our sacred humanness. May we invite forth the grace of being who we are together.

Who Will Hear a Who?

There's a well-known children's book written by Dr. Seuss entitled *Horton Hears a Who*. In it Horton, an elephant, finds a tiny flower seed upon which an entire population of Who's live. Throughout the story, Horton affirms what he feels and intuits. He becomes the courageous and tender protector for the Who's existence because he believes in what he's experiencing. No one in his community recognizes or hears the teeny tiny Who's, so Horton validates what his outer world doesn't support. His community cannot hear or value the sounds of anything they cannot see.

Through heroic efforts to protect this 'smaller' existence from the 'bigger' one of his peers, Horton calls the Who's en masse to make greater noise than they've ever done before. Horton implores every single Who in Whoville to use their voice to be heard so they will not be destroyed. And the Who's come squeaking, whispering, singing, screaming...

And when the tiniest of all Who's comes forward and blows his horn, Horton's outer world *hears* the inner one of the Who's. And they begin to believe in each other.

The way of our creative feminine is like this. Intrinsically designed into the caverns of our 'smallest', most infinitesimal, unimaginable existence lives the deepest honoring of all life. Science has revealed that the tinier something is there is more measurable empty space within it. As we rest in this, we loosen judgments and cultural proclivities to see the world through big and small, important and unimportant, or valuable and of no value. As we stop trying to fill everything up out of fear of our own emptiness, we learn its deeper importance and our own.

We are filled with empty space so we can create and grow life from within it. And this is where our true preciousness resides. By honoring the smallest aspect within us, creates more space to honor the grandness of all. This isn't about honoring one over the other. It's about honoring that we are designed to be in collaboration. We need each other to become all we can be. When we listen to what lives within, all are heard.

There is a quote that sits above my workspace I refer to often to remind me of what is most important to my soul.

> *When the animals come to us, asking for our*
> *help, will we know what they are saying?*
> *When the plants speak to us, in their delicate, beautiful*
> *language, will we be able to answer them?*
> *When the planet herself sings to us in our dreams,*
> *will we be able to wake ourselves and act?*
>
> ~ Gary Lawless

On this path of discovering our feminine presence and creative wisdom, we can feel as if we've been living 'too small'. Feminine wisdom is a soft, subtle existence. It is flowing and fluid, melting in to the next contour and shift. This inner encompassing has and can take a back seat as our culture and recent history has invalidated it, focusing on a defined, structured, easily tangible experience of our masculine directive. The outer world of external progress and proclamation, of being able to measure and show all we've accomplished and created, becomes the path for revealing our worth and value. Yet this is not what will take us to the depths, truths and transformation of humanity's well-being. It only creates more and more of an obsessive outer search for fulfillment.

Our transformation begins within our smallest, darkest, most immeasurable and unknowable selves. Within what we've shamed and felt ashamed of because the outer world has not defined the value it carries. As we begin a path of self-valuing the unseeable within, life has an opportunity to transform its belief. Through our feminine restoration we value our beauty, shape, wisdom and its form, irrespective of the sound and quality, or other external measurements.

In our infinitesimal nature we are so grand.

Externally enlarging how we live does not bring us to the threshold of valuing our inner existence. Enlarging our awareness of the empty space within shifts how we feel in the world. A mutual reaction within our sense of inner/outer reality begins. Nothing along the way will be lost. Our sense of inner value brings outer value to life.

In the move towards valuing a 'smaller' or more simplified existence, people have gone to great measures to simplify and declutter their lives. Yet attempting to only simplify the external measures of our lives will not 'clear the inner closets'. Things will keep piling up in our psyches. We will forget to appreciate the beauty, color and way in which we express ourselves through the matter of our world. We simplify our outer world of clutter by adjusting the internal excess we believe about our worth in the world. This allows us to see and hear what is no longer needed in our environment. These internal measures transform our external lives. We grow harmonious with the well-being of our souls as we honor our personal value and what it provides for the whole.

Inside each of us exists countless flower seeds. And there are endless Who's living upon them! We have an opportunity and the reward of finding out what each speck of our existence offers. Like Horton who enters a field filled with endless flower seeds to find the lost one upon which the Who's live, our journey goes through all we need to discover the value of our existence. At times it may appear simply daunting. Yet our feminine wisdom is not bound by size or fueled from our exhaustion. An embryo holds the complete possibility for life, and the knowledge of the cosmos and blueprint of its ancestry. It will endure through endless extremes to support life being born. We can trust what we hear, feel and intuit. We can become courageous protectors of the smallest realms within our being. We can make noise... so tender, so heartfelt. We will be heard.

And by who?

May we come to value how important it is to hear ourselves... our tiniest heartbeat, our quietest dreams, our soundless whispers, our deepest longings.

To know the wisdom of what cannot be seen has far more value than our outer-based existence has upheld. This is a path of honoring smallness, and dissolving any dichotomy that big and small is in opposition. To follow the feminine creativity of our soul is to celebrate that which cannot be seen, proven or even made tangible from the outside. This is an inner pathway of carving a container for the depth, wealth and abundance naturally intrinsic within us all. This is about trust and faith, about being the beacon of what lives within. We become Carriers of the Who.

As we embrace the insides of ourselves, we share and live its emanation. We become the expression of a world that exists beyond or is bound by size. The path of creative expression does not know about being too little or too big. Its purpose is to honor it all.

Offering Her Gifts

It is often said after a woman has a child her heart now walks around outside of her.

This is what occurs as a woman opens to share her deepest gifts with the world. And this is the barricade that suddenly erects as a woman gets close to opening her heart-womb wisdom, causing many to turn back. The choice to not go forth in the world expressing who one truly is, is as important as the choice to go forth. It holds information and riches more valuable than we've been willing to listen to and face.

In modern society, the choice to not express ourselves in some 'big' way has been labeled as 'living small,' often seen with negative connotations attached. Yet what if this is the exact message our culture longs to hear and learn more about?

What if, like in *Horton Hears a Who* even though few have been able to see and hear the value of what hasn't been said and seen, doesn't make it any less important? We choose to live small for important reasons. We feel our world doesn't know or respect what we've carried within. This *is* following our intuition.

This *is* listening to creation's timing versus our single-minded orchestration of it. And this message is more vital for humanity's well-being than we've ever let on.

This creates a challenging dichotomy within a woman, as she senses something from within holding her expression in, yet also feels drawn outward to offer something to the world. This is why many women currently feel bound up, as if they're betraying themselves or the world. They just cannot win. This results in symptoms on the physical, social, emotional, health, financial and relational plane, that are often seen as disharmonious or unhealthy. Each of us exemplifies areas that are not in balance within the whole of our society. By being with these feelings and the sensation of this inner/outer struggle, the self or world dichotomy, a woman learns to mother her heart and her most tender inner landscape. She discovers her wisdom and learns to live by it. She sets herself free from carrying the weight and pain of the world.

Creating and sharing from her deepest wisdom is what creates internal balance within a woman's body and sense of value. The feminine is housed in the internal landscape inside us all... it breathes through the organs we cannot see, through the chambers of the heart beating below the surface, through the pathways of our soul we may never make tangible. With the societal emphasis on outer expression, what has been unexpressed and inexpressible gets devalued. Yet its value and worth is not connected to our expression of it. What is sacred will never be limited to what we think or say we are.

We've believed we've lived small, like a Who, until we discover the strength and perseverance of Horton the elephant within us. As we allow this energy to bring worth to what we know is alive, vital and thriving within our nature, we go forth sharing our true song. We become the valiant protector of our authenticity and sincerity, of our greatest tenderness and vulnerability, learning to craft and share these 'smallest' or inconsequential experiences with the world. We hold value for life moments that move us profoundly without explanation. We treasure the sublime and mundane and don't let outer definitions of worth rob us of what *we* feel or can explain. We learn to not take on another's perspective or judgments about what is sacred, precious and valuable. Through our own gifts we define, craft and form what is as vital to life as our breath is within us.

In my fifteen plus years working in the field of women's spirituality and fulfillment, I've experienced this directly and seen it time and again with those I've sat with. The terror of knowing that your most tender parts and pieces will be exposed to the criticisms and perspectives of others, can be more than most can bear. And yet it is through sharing our creative vulnerabilities that we come to an enduring sense of peace within. As a woman is willing to be seen in her vulnerability and wisdom, she allows herself to see who she is. Through this process, her relationships, especially with those she holds most dear, experience a new sense of fulfillment and healing. The feminine is honored and the pathway of inherent creation is set free. She stands with a rose in her hands inviting the whole world to see the beauty and worth of her deepest heart.

Unbreakable Connection

As I write this, a year has passed since these Life Artists and I set off on our *Faces of the Mother* journey. At the onset of our creative undertaking I traveled to the ocean to initiate, receive, bless and bestow this process and our personal unfolding. It was July 22, 2013, Mary Magdalene's feast day.

Exactly a year later I sit at the computer, in awe at the close-to-complete manuscript resting in my hands. I could never have constructed this synchronistic rhythm or the events that occurred between them. I could never have known the sacred orchestration of this unfolding. I am not in this alone, and all of life has supported me. I can listen and remember. I am blessed to engage the creative fertility of my soul when I feel drawn to craft and play. This magnificent and attainable force lives inside us all.

A year ago I went with my family to the coast, offering the heart of this journey into the ocean and to the Great Mother. A year later my family has just left for the coast, offering me, a great mother, a weekend to myself to complete this commitment in the ocean of my being.

As my husband and sons prepared to leave for the beach this morning, I snuggled with my youngest. This will be our longest duration apart. We've been separate from each other for a night only two times before. I place my hand upon his heart and remind him where my love lives. We speak of finding me here if he feels sad or alone. I share how our connection is unbreakable, not bound by being together physically. I let him know I will be waiting for his return.

All weekend this conversation swells inside me as I savor undisturbed hours for writing, not doing dishes, listening to music and watching movies. I don't get dressed or make the bed. Relishing this other side of my home life and self, I feel this unbreakable connection I hold within. This connection is not bound to what I do or how I do it. It is not intertwined with who I think I am, who I am with and what they think of me. This connection is my enduring legacy from the source of my life. It has never been touched by anything but my own sincerity. I rest my hand on my heart and womb. I breathe into my body through all that I am.

This creative soul connection is what orchestrated our *Faces of the Mother* process. It is what oversees and crafts the daily movement of our lives. As we trust its presence we show up for life from a deepened perspective and resilient inner crafting, knowing we're united with humanity through all of our days.

As I step away from writing and the computer, and venture outside to water our garden, I reflect further on this connection. At our home we water most everything by hand. It is a time-consuming yet delicious ritual for me, walking around the yard peering at all that is growing. Noticing the subtlest, smallest, most intimate changes. As the water flows from the hose I say a blessing, knowing these flowers and plants are teachers for how creation actually unfolds. I watch them closely.

I move to the area in our yard where we've buried many of our animal companions. We live on a small urban farm in the city. Here we raise chickens and ducks, house bees and have many domestic pets. Over the years we've held space for the transition of lots of our animals. My boys and I have painted memory stones with each animal's name on them in bright colors to honor their eternal place in our hearts and their unbreakable connection to our family. As I water the plants in this area I feel tender. The energy of our cat, Onyx, who passed away last year during our *Faces of the Mother* process encircles me. He is the one that the Feminine Life Artist sensed the morning we spoke on the phone.

I reach down and rinse off each painted stone. My heart is full with my life.

Oftentimes we don't realize how creative, rich and rewarding our lives are until something has been lost or we've stepped away from its everyday reality. As my boys and husband are gone this weekend, I feel how much I appreciate them and their idiosyncrasies. I feel how special our family connection is.

I remember the animals we've lost and feel a profound relationship with each one and the sacred blessings their lives have bestowed on my journey.

I reflect on this past year moving through and transcribing the voyage I've taken with these Life Artists. I feel the unbreakable connection beyond words flow through my body and heart.

We live in eternal connection.

We can trust and be grateful for this as we make our way through twists and turns in crafting our life. What comes in and flows through us is all precious. It is also the greatest heroism we will face as we find our unique and imperative way. Breathing soft and full into my belly I remember what is eternal, giving thanks for this fertile connection to the source of love. It lives here, in the soil I am watering. It lives here, in the soul of my life.

Faces of the Mother is a tender depiction of blessed and challenging moments. It reminds me of a butterfly one of my boys once captured so he could get close and watch it in his net. My son grew intimate with its beauty. He became humble as its captor. He seemed to know he'd let the butterfly go and didn't ask for direction. He inherently understood the well-being of the butterfly depended on his choice.

Through letting go we feel how sacred our creations are. In sharing them with others we come to understand how significant our lives are to the whole. By setting life free we see the power that rests in our own hands.

I recently closed down the womb sanctuary and office space I'd been working in for the past 5 years. With four other women we'd created a modern day temple housed in a historic Masonic Lodge, to share and gather in celebration of our gifts and feminine wisdom. This is the place the Feminine Life Artists and I gathered in celebration of the *Faces of the Mother* process almost 9 months ago. As I packed my belongings from there, I paused to gaze at 2 art pieces the Artists gifted me. I could not have known they would be traveling home with me, blessing this next stage of my creative work, honoring my home as a living sanctuary. The art pieces now hang in my living room. One of them is a cocoon... the womb of feminine regeneration. The other is a Priestess.

Even as we let the butterfly and the bird fly free, our connection to it never leaves us. Making the choice to live in the freedom of our creative expression is an honor and celebration of this unbreakable connection. We give it visibility and voice to restore humanity's and our own feminine well-being. This is a sacred opportunity to let go of the constraints, peel away the masks, and take down any barriers to all that stands in the way of our intimacy with the Mother and ourselves. Here we learn we are each a complete treasure.

As one of the Life Artists moved through a tender process, allowing greater depth and transparency for her expressive freedom, she learned how to release the butterfly from its net. Here she shares her gratitude and discovery, "It's an opportunity to say a deeper goodbye. And ask for the blessing of these women artists, their support and their faces of the mother, in loving witness to my struggle to let go of the mask the mother has worn. Down the road, I can see that this will be the point I felt myself turn into the light, and that turning became a natural movement."

Peeling Away the Mask... face of our Feminine wisdom

It happened suddenly. As I typed the last section for this book's manuscript, my uterus and cervical tissue began to shift and prolapsed.

For years I've worked energetically and physically with my pelvic care, healing and strengthening the ligaments around my internal organs. I've birthed 3 babes vaginally, one of them close to 13 lbs. My body has known love, otherworldly power and intense fear and resistance. The practice of greeting, facing and working with shame in connection to my feminine wisdom, expression and body has been a life long process. I trust it has no end.

The passage through pregnancy, birth, creating and raising life is an act of grace and service, the kind our culture and selves still know so little about truly revering. As waves of emotion pass through my softening uterus, eons of shame slip away. The uterus is our physical and energetic storehouse for our feminine creativity. It is the container and home of our soul's fertility. I breathe, placing a hand here. The story I've carried of the feminine no longer will be housed in the confines I've constructed or been told.

Along this new passage She feels the breeze blowing. She roams in the wilds, untethered and unnamed. The folds of my skin and layers of tissue cannot even contain Her. Through me She chooses to sit where She will, however She will. She is wild and dark. She is bright and bestows blessings. She is tender and abiding. She is etheric and not of the body. She chooses a life of chaos and order, of connection and isolation. She hangs loose and turns inward. Her house comes alive through my crafting and is supported by the whole of the universe.

In the early hours of the morn I sit with Her, breathing wide into the mask I have worn to hide from the full force of my power. I enter this domain where I am open and vulnerable, longing to know Her deepest truth and message.

I am the temple of your creativity. Through the folds of my flesh you become the artist of your life, flowing and feeling, fashioning and forming out of the dynamic of my inner territory. Babies come into being through me. All of your projects, masterpieces, expressions and stories are brought to life through the territory of my container. Honoring this has no end.

Within my network of skin and tissue, blood and muscle, I serve one purpose and one purpose only, to bring forth and gestate the beauty of your life. The joy I know in having built and grown the visions of your dreams is my deepest pleasure and fulfillment.

The shrine of your woman's temple is my chamber. I sit poised at center to orchestrate all directions of your creative life. Whether you realize this does not prevent it from being so. And when you grow in realization of this, you build the altar of your life from within the matter of your own nature.

Shame, resentment and regret tear away at the resiliency of my function and fluidity. Yet nothing you believe, can do or have done, will prevent the sacredness of my purpose and form.

Forgive yourself. Forgive yourself.

*Forgive your sense of unworthiness. Forgive the world of all demoralization.
Forgive all that has been and gone before. Forgive all that is to come.*

*In the blink of an eye I am restored through your vision into all that
I already am. It takes your clarity and certainty to craft the truth
of your life through your Feminine way. Trust this process.*

I adore you.

~ A MESSAGE FROM MY UTERUS

☙

She awakens through my body and shows me the home I will never leave or
abandon. Like the wisdom of my grandmothers who knew a humble surrender
of their physical form, I release. Through the initiation of aging, of walking this
path that celebrates my humanity, I breathe into and with this experience. I touch
the small space at the base of my spine, rubbing my lower back. This area begins
to tighten and grow sore. I remember contractions in labor I've experienced here.
They anchored me to the earth's core. They were a focal point, where my notions
of spirit and body as separate wrangled and fought for who would lead the way.
Knowing union was inevitable during birthing, I remained present, tethered to
my heart, humanity and self through each wave rippling across my back.

I now call forth the words from a dear friend's song I repeated as a mantra
through my third son's labor, "I will do the labor if it sets my sisters free. Yes!
I will do the labor if it sets my sisters free."[1] I release and let go knowing there
is nothing I need to hold up or onto. I am not in this alone. I am present to the
wild unknown of this path of the feminine body and our legacy of sisterhood. It
takes me to unmatched pleasure and into terrain I can only wail through.

---

1   Omiza River, How You Livin,' http://omizariver.com/

There is nothing to resist, hold up or onto. I breathe. I let go. Her power is my own and it has no limitations. My prayer is given to the earth as my uterus descends into Her care.

Dearest Uterus, Holy Chalice of your grace, aid me in and through this passage. Help me humbly proclaim my own forgiveness as the walls of my heart, womb and life come crashing down. May I not fear the ability to walk away from it all... from the notions I've held about what this means, and the judgments I've erected of my own inherent value. May I let go. May I surrender everything into your infallible care.

It is you that holds me up. It is you that gives me breath, life and the tender fortitude to carry on. It is you that sees me live through my wounding and patterns over and over again, and still believes in all that I am without such notions. And I know it is you that will carry me to the threshold of my next doorway. Here I am forever home.

Thank you for loving me. Thank you for showing me that no matter what, I am held in your care. I know you don't wish for me to struggle; yet you will not stop my choice to experience it. I know you don't wish for me to live in pain; yet you will not stop my choice to have it. I know you wish not for me to feel separate from you; yet you will not prevent me from believing this is true.

I hold the inner chambers of my body and creativity up to your light, plan and purpose. I tenderly accept the deeper throes of my dreams. Through me they can be made real. May the path be clear. Help me choose my next step. And then the one after that. Breathe me into utter honesty of where I am and where I can be. Help me walk my way, opening to you and the wisdom you are willing to pour forth through my form.

May I treasure this. May I share it with the world.

~ A PRAYER TO MY SACRED UTERUS

My gifts are shared through whatever is to come. As the temple of my creativity slips down the caverns of my body's threshold to life, I honor what I cannot know. Over the past few weeks I've felt the energy of the pushing stage I experienced during my last son's birth.

With my first two pregnancies a lip on my cervix slipped down during labor as I worked with spirit to usher my babes into this life. My struggle heightened, as it didn't seem to matter how much I pushed or exerted effort. This unknown fold of skin blocked my boys' heads from continuing along the birth canal. These laboring transitions were long and painful, tiring on my body and strength. My birth team was initially confused about what was going on. I subconsciously walked away from these experiences believing I didn't know how to engage with the creative forces of the universe for manifestation. I believed my efforts did not matter.

With my third son's birth all this changed. I listened throughout pregnancy to the womb and inner pathway of my being and to his spirit against all odds. In labor my son descended through my body in less than fifteen minutes. No cervical lip protruded. I pushed like a wild woman, knowing no limit to my strength and determination. I remember the light that went on during that experience. It revealed how I inherently know how to engage with the creative forces of life. It was direct and imperative to honor it for what only I could explain. It was a tangible experience of how I live in co-creation, mutuality and sacred timing.

I now find out what's descending through my body is this lip of my cervix. It's an anatomical uniqueness, how my body is normal and different. The gynecologist described it as the hood on a baseball cap. Mine is extra long. I sense it reflects how I peer deeply into life and spirit, revealing the sacred through all that we are.

In my third son's pregnancy I regularly received Bowen treatments, a type of bodywork that restores natural alignment. My practitioner, and a dear friend, affirmed my normalcy and uniqueness, sharing how what I was going through and how I was experiencing it was always normal for me. We are all differently designed. We are each perfect. Our bodies are the living expression of immense wisdom and grace for the creative template of ourselves through life.

Soothing our feminine essence and reminding her that her form, no matter what, is pure and sacred, is paramount in a culture that exemplifies and rigidly defines beauty, fulfillment, success and health through stringent, one-size-fits-all expressions. The sacred nature of ourselves is not contained in the limited ways we construct our sense of reality and life. We are wise whether we have all our body parts or not. We are beautiful no matter our size. We flourish whether we are scarred, maimed or disfigured. We are holy just as we are.

You can wrap your arms around the collective daughters of this world and let them know their true beauty is more than skin deep.

~ KRISIEY, OUR HEALER

What once felt like it blocked my creative capacity and even hurt my babes in labor, now extends forth to open my way. I trust this. Over the past three weeks I've remembered this experience of my third son's labor as my life, body, creation's power and sacred timing all worked harmoniously together. Only I can know the path of life and its manifestation through me. I breathe in all that is to be born.

Creation's Timing

I could not have understood time's sacred relevance and natural unfolding without the experience I had through my sons' births. I would not have truly believed that time supports and upholds our deeper longings and growth without this sense of 'being held back' from manifesting.

What occurred in my labors was not my only experience of feeling ready at the gate while the bars delayed opening. As a child my family was known for 'late arrivals'. I was the youngest of four girls. It was an effort to get everyone out the door, especially each Sunday to attend church. I remember how flushed my face would feel as we entered the sanctuary and attempted to find an open pew to sit in. The pattern of 'being late' was something I struggled with into my adulthood.

Until we heal this relationship with what we've known and experienced as 'time', we cannot embrace creation's natural timing through us and our lives. We will see time and the unfolding of our dreams through a distorted perspective, one in which we are either in charge of or at fault for, until we directly feel the seamless way all things move in sacred orchestration. To heal my understanding of time I honored my way of feminine manifestation. I looked at the underlying judgments I carried that "I was always late." I saw how hard I worked to fit into other people's time, notions and vision. I settled in to the still point of my own perfect timing, and held this in the core of my womb. I began to be 'on time.' As I experienced this, I learned it had little to do with a clock and more to do with respecting and enjoying time with and for myself.

We naturally carry big visions and long to bring them to fruition. We are dreamers creating new ways of living and relating. Often we erect detailed pictures and life stories of what it is we believe we want. We then work towards this, breaking the larger vision into bite-size pieces, creating dream boards and setting New Year intentions. These steps offer tangibility so we can see and believe in what we long for. This is important to the journey of growing intimate with the texture of time throughout our lives.

Yet we will be taken by time's tender hand upon a passage we cannot predict, into the cycles of our unique and personal unfolding. Here we will touch the places of our most soulful nature in support of the legacy of ourselves coming forth. We can create just to create, and we must learn where our creations come from. Through this process we get to touch the source of creativity within ourselves, and allow all our creations to be imbued with grace's timelessness.

As we rest face-to-face with the energy of creation's time, we discover a unique brand of our own and the deeper purpose to the inherent timing of our lives. We learn to not resist how we personally grow. And begin to joyously create out of such intimacy as our expression lights up our soul. This impacts the world in ways beyond what we could ever imagine or need to. These creations feel like no effort, no matter how much time we've put in. In a moment of completion, it is like no time has passed. As we hold the creations of our timeless soul in our hands, it's like looking into the eyes of a newborn babe, recognizing we've known one another for all time. Notions of 'waiting' dissipate; time becomes inconsequential and utterly aligned.

The flow of time is a sacred expression of the passage of our lives. It honors Feminine and Masculine energies, and offers texture and tangibility to the cycles of co-creation, our individuated selves and inter-relational existence. Creation's timing is not from our linear world, yet it moves through it to balance and clarify the fluidity of life. Like the movement of winter into spring, we witness time through plants and trees reflecting subtle and seasonal changes. They receive information through their direct relationship with the earth and skies... through their roots, how much sun or rain there is, and the effects of the environment. Time honors the many layers of our co-existence, from the soil below us to the planets in the far galaxies. In creation's time all is intermingling. There is a seamless blessing flowing through time's orchestration whose gifts are not for a select few. They are for every aspect of life.

We've used time as a tool to chart the course of history and find a common point to come together. We've crafted and constructed ways to work with and express time, forming it into something we can monitor, track and contain. Yet holy timing is uncontainable. It bleeds into the next moment, season and year. It reveals we are creatures of rhythm and congruency, following the prompts of our natural and inner world, cosmos, family patterns, ancient lineage and culture. Even when we are not aware of the impact of these forces, they will guide our way, becoming ever more apparent.

For years I've charted the personal energies of my year, noting patterns of sadness and apathy, of vitality and energy, of the longing to draw in and the desire to connect out.

At one point I noticed the hardest time of my life fell on the same day in mid-April. I began to hold this in my awareness and through simple ceremony honored the grief I experienced at this time each year. Eventually I learned both my husband's father and my maternal grandfather passed away on this day. It was also my maternal grandmother's birthday. My mother was 16 when her father unexpectedly died. My husband was 26 when his father passed away from cancer. Now I write 'lineage honoring' on this day on my calendar. I revere the wisdom and healing that comes through creation's time into my life. I trust I will know what needs to be made known in its own sacred timing.

Creation's timing is noticeable yet indefinable. We can honor the time we encapsulate through our calendars and clocks, along with the otherworldly rhythms weaving it all together. As any woman who's been pregnant knows, timing takes on its own sense of order as a mother experiences cycles of gestation, birth and parenting. Any parent with a newborn babe feels how the constructs of day and night have no distinction.

Feminine Pacing

The landscape of our feminine creativity follows an inner pacing that does not always correlate with the outer and modern world's sense of time. Manifestation follows cycles and rhythms. It has outward and productive times, and inward and retreat times. These periods can be visibly seen and noticed on the surface, while also living underground in unseen domains.

To work with feminine pacing, we engage our faith and awareness in the unseeable or 'bigger picture', while celebrating the present moment and smaller movements of our life that we can touch, taste and feel. In bringing forward our dreams, we delve in to the recesses of our hearts, following them into our bellies, discovering a texture for our purpose and a connection to these seeds unfolding. As *Faces of the Mother* attests, we cannot know the details or particulars of how something will unfold, yet we can feel, trust and follow from deep in our bones what we are designed for, allowing the attraction of our soul's fertility to magnetically pull towards us all that will benefit.

Manifestation has been portrayed as something we can individually control. It's been upheld as a pathway to getting/creating what you want. True manifestation is about *becoming* who you are. When you travel to the internal recesses of your own nature, you discover that being who you are IS what you most want! You become a conscious integral aspect of the creative process expressing itself each step of the way.

There are many interrelated factors, as in a family, that engage the unfolding of creation. One person does not control or dictate how creation unfolds. We are drawn together to serve creation and are served through it. We are each a tuning fork for this one main purpose we are all working towards. Each of us can more consciously attune and listen to life's unfolding to aid us in finding our expressive way. Our personal dreams will not be lost. They are for the good of all.

A feminine way of timing follows the deeper nature of the earth, moon and seasonal cycles. A woman moves in tune with these larger forces and cosmological patterns as she breathes into a place of acceptance for herself and the way she was naturally created. She listens to her body, honors her blood, welcomes her feelings and embraces her pain. These cornerstones aid us in returning to and remaining deeply intimate with the feminine pacing of our dreams. Supporting us through the fallow times, and through the inward descent into seasons of our symbolic 'winter' when it appears as if nothing is happening in the outer realms. The wisdom of our feminine nature knows what a mother knows. It is *these* times, when all on the surface appears asleep or at rest, that the most vital growth and transformation is occurring to bring vitality forth for all to behold.

We cannot control the parameters of time, yet we can sense and intuit the seasons of our lives and creative fertility. We can feel the cycles of inward and outward inclinations and work with them. We can trust when things don't come together as we envisioned, its essence and seed has *already* traveled into our being and into tender relationship with our source. It will take all the time it requires to surface and reveal. We are an integral aspect of the whole. Here nothing is forgotten. What WILL reveal is the complete truth of our own hearts. As it is born, we may not initially recognize its face and form, yet as a parent tending its well-being each step of the way, we will come to recognize it's an integral part of us and has always been so. We will embrace it in soulful homecoming.

Our culture's directive, linear focus on time has squelched our deeper intuitive understanding about the larger systems at play through the creative process. The world now rides on timing related to production, export and demand, leaving little to no space for restoring our spirit and deeper creative impulse, and being at peace with our entropy. Watching the cycles of a garden and its plants, we learn about creation's timing and cultivation. Tending the garden, we grow humble to Sacred Feminine manifestation.

May we become saturated in the abiding wisdom of creation's time and feminine pacing, welcoming what is unfolding through and around us now.

Medicine of the Feminine

To support me through these shifts of my body, uterus and cervix, I reach out to connect with my mother. This inherent longing to connect with her often arises as I face deep issues in my fertility, mothering, changing identity and softening heart. The healing work and wisdom I've trained in, taught and directly experienced with the relationship we hold with our mothers helps me anchor these next steps for my growth and care.

Our connection to our mothers holds the energy of our core wounding and most vibrant creative patterns. Through it we can learn how we show up to life and allow life to flow through us. This primary relationship of mother-child holds the treasures of the universe. In its healing and seeing it for what it actually is, we open the doorway we all long to pass through. Here we face the truth about who we are and who the Mother is, growing real, forgiving and tender to our power and humanity as co-creators with the sacred in form.

On the phone I feel more vulnerable with my mother than I have in awhile. I know this means I'm being honest with myself. I share what's happening in my body. I give voice to the ancient longing of my feminine innocence. My mother feels helpless. She wishes she could help me, to make the pain go away. When my mother asks how she can help, I invite her to show me how to love myself. I ask her to role model her power so I might learn about my own. I acknowledge I wish she'd taught me how strong and special I was. I honor that these feelings of helplessness are hers. I do not ask for our pain to go away. I let soft tears flow.

My mother was a homemaker. She was a creator of this Sacred Feminine foundation, yet little did she know how valuable her role and wisdom were. Little did she take in the immensity of what she was offering to her family and our world. She grew up in the 1950's; her surrounding culture didn't reflect the life-giving service that Mother and Home provide for us all. Right after birthing me, the youngest of 4 daughters, my mother's uterus was removed.

In closing our conversation, my mother suggests I wrap the shawl around me she sent while I was pregnant with my last son. Knitted amongst a circle of women from her church, they'd sincerely prayed on my behalf. In the lineage of women's sacred medicine, they offered blessings into the yarn and its weave for a safe passage through that pregnancy and for the medical conditions I was experiencing. I understand how my mother and our culture devalued the medicine of the feminine. Her prayers, in circle amongst sisters, rooted in feminine faith and the power of the heart and connection to each other has always been greater than we've let on. A woman's sacred wisdom and inherent medicine transforms everything around her.

I claim the value of this healing and feminine wisdom now. I breathe. On the phone I ask my mother if she realized how powerful her prayers were. I let her know I am grateful for what she's bestowing upon me.

I can feel something between us shift and know our mother-daughter beauty is being restored.

It may not look like I envisioned it would. I, too, was impacted by the messages of my culture. As a young woman who struggled with wanting more than her mother had, I did not know how to accept the deepest value of my mother's feminine medicine each time she offered it. I visualize the shawl draped around me and breathe in its gifts and grace.

A few weeks ago during the closing ceremony I held at my womb sanctuary and workspace, one woman responded to our opening question, "What do you hate about yourself?" Through soft tears she stated, "That I haven't been a good friend to my mother." She was a *Faces of the Mother* Life Artist!

I hold this understanding close to my heart. I am here to love my mother as I love the mother within me. I receive my mother's adoration, from above and below, from afar and right within. I will wrap the shawl of blue-hued yarn around me ever tighter.

As we say goodbye on the phone, my mother tells me to keep the faith. I feel her wisdom running deep through me.

Into the Core... moving with and beyond the body

The journey of feminine reclamation and working with the art of your life's creations is one that takes you into the body to find that you can reach beyond and through it to offer our bodies and life experience in service to the whole.

This passage takes us to the throes of our distinct nature. Into our most holy physical caverns to see there is nothing of this world that can contain us, and everything within this world that will reflect us. This is liberating for our feminine expression. It is maddening for our masculine sense of order. And within the core of ourselves we find a union that harmonizes such polar distinctions so we can craft and create from our purest wholeness. This is the gift of being human and expressing our sacred passion.

Since childhood I've easily found myself connected to my spirit, riding beyond the boundaries of my form. I've also cherished and enjoyed my body and physicality, dancing, swimming, biking, walking and growing intimate with the earth. I've gardened barefoot for so long my father claims my feet look like his grandmothers did!

This journey is not about choosing the body over the spirit, or the soul over the flesh. It is not about feeling you must live solely in isolation or in community, or pick having a family over sharing vibrant individual work. This is our gentle return to the wonder that lives within, and allowing that to show us how we uniquely find our way into the simplicity of this moment and life. Within us lives the infinitesimal existence of creation's beginning and end. Within us is forged our ability to live at the heart of life.

These are poetic declarations and scientifically proven realities. Yet any need for external validation falls away as we venture into the creativity within. Through internal reorientation, we validate what is real. A point will come when science, spirituality, religion, education and nature reveal the same basic truths and discoveries. We are getting close! And at that point we'll no longer strive for outer validation, but will reveal inner celebration through these forms of our unique genius and devotion.

This is a mutual journey. As long as individuals and the collective yearn for outer definition and proof of our value, we will create systems to do that and they will contradict. When we travel within to personally discover the place where all things come from one common source, this will no longer be necessary. Our experience of outer opposition will begin to dissolve.

To become a Feminine Life Artist is like being delicately opened so we can see we are seated in our core, and thus refine and rebuild the beauty of our body from the intrinsic value we hold for all life within. In doing this we show up to the form of our gifts so they can shape and be offered in their most refined and impactful possibility. We become the writers, painters, poets, singers, sculptors, dancers, lovers, mothers and fathers, sisters and brothers we've longed to be. And we no longer care how it looks or unfolds. This isn't an act of apathy. It is surrender to and reliance upon our natural grace.

As more and more of our society and people treasure themselves and their inherently bestowed craft, we free the world to appreciate itself for who it is, how it looks and is designed to be. Such notions of big and little, ugly and pretty, fat or thin, white or black, artistic or not, good or bad, melt into something indefinable, while still being sacredly distinguishable and respected. Here the comparisons no longer hold. We stop the struggle to express what cannot be expressed. In this place we do not force ourselves to be something we are not. We see all that we are, and that is enough.

May we open our hearts wide to offer what only we can through each of our moments, knowing it has significance.

Sacred Life Artistry

The *Faces of the Mother* collection was initiated and pursued inside each woman through her own life story and longing to express herself authentically in this world.

Through the unfolding of our journey we began to see the embodiment of a Mother coming alive in each woman, irrespective if she had birthed children or not. Moving ever deeper into what was essential for each woman as an artist, we witnessed what she most valued in her life, heart, for her soul and the soul of the world. This was what I initially hoped would occur... that each woman might live into and from her Mother Face, feeling its wisdom intimately guiding her. Through this I sensed we might come to understand what it is that blocks us from seeing and being fully ourselves in each moment. *Faces of the Mother* has become the expression of what is true and possible as we deeply trust, engage and create from our inner feminine fertility.

Along this adventure I knew we couldn't hold attachment to what would be the end result of this project or for each artist. This was about being Feminine Life Artists. We are the creative artists of our lives and can choose to give that credit and sacred expression. Many of our artists experienced a shocking transformation from the original vision they held of their Mother Face. Several Faces were painted over as new ones took form. Creative mediums originally felt to be the one that would express a Face changed. One woman envisioned a collage or painting, and then moved into writing a poem. One artist felt she'd be painting, and then was intuitively drawn to take pictures, becoming a photographer in the process. Another artist envisioned quillwork on paper and through her process awakened as the living face, realizing she didn't need to create anything externally at all. She was and is life's greatest artistic creation.

And so it is with this book. Here we weave our story all the way back to its inception, holding a tender bird in our hands, knowing it is meant to fly. We cannot know the trajectory of its course. It may fall to the ground and be eaten by a predator. It may tip from its nest high in the tree to be picked up by tender hands that beg a mother to care for and safeguard it until it can fly. This bird may fly higher and faster into the vast sky, setting its own course. It may be a bird of flock that finds its winged passage amongst the formation of many.

Irrespective of what will or has occurred, the creative process reveals we must let go, take a step, move forth, onward and from our stillness. And then we will be invited to let go again and again, cycling through all over again.

We can feel with our hearts and sense with our wombs what is right for us each step of the way. None of it will ever be wrong. This is our flight and our fall. It is our time to soar and to descend. We need not judge the passage or how and where it will go. It is all ripe for creation revealing and us seeing we are the tender hands this newborn bird rests in. It is time to trust ourselves. It is time to trust our lives.

And it is up to us how we let go and hold on. How we listen to the wind and ways of the natural world. How we gently touch this bird's downy feathers and whisper how much it is adored. Through our hands the next moment is created.

Wisdom of Love

These pages you've journeyed through exhibit triumph of spirit, endurance of faith and belief in the inner capacity of our humanity to create beauty and blessing out of the delicate and intrinsic moments of our lives, however chaotic, fluid, gentle, grace-filled and brash they seem. This is the power of the Mother instilled in us. *Faces of the Mother* exhibits perseverance and commitment to the truth of who we are and what ignites our passion. This is how we grow into our Feminine Life Artistry.

We each are collaborative Life Artists of the sacred reality of our lives. This journey and our *Faces of the Mother* expressions reflect an incomprehensible wisdom. This collection is comprised of unique, important glimpses, radiant and pure. Here we offer that which can only be experienced through one's own being. Are you willing to give everything to love and step forth in its embrace? Please know you will be ready in the way that only you can be.

Faces of the Mother is an ever-enduring invitation. Join us now and again, in the many Faces of Her that live within. As we do, we grow intimate and connected to the rich tapestry of creation coming alive within us all.

How much we've forgotten our own intrinsic worth, value and sacred capacity to create life now and forevermore is testament to what it will take to move into becoming a Feminine Life Artist of your own wondrous creation. As you live through your heart and womb you come to see what you hold, we all long for. Will you accept this invitation and join us in its crafting? Will you surrender into Her and thus into your deepest self... and then do it all over again?

We pray to you, for we know She dwells within your soul.
We pray for you, for we know She is born through your being.
We pray with you, for we know you are our reflection.
We pray, for we know we are Her children
falling in love with ourselves within Her grace.

ॐ

Voice of the Voiceless... gratitude for it all

*'Let It Be' ringing in my ears — the complete knowing that I am on
my journey in this creative study we are beginning. Love, Sarah*

~ SARAH, OUR DISTILLER

Writing this book has required my commitment to and appreciation for union and community... allowing inner and outer connections to support me in releasing notions of separation and revealing what is alive and well between us all.

After supporting these Feminine Life Artists, my journey kicked in full swing as my own exploration of creativity and the deeper life of the Mother was reignited. Through my willingness to walk beside, as and with these women through what they faced and went through, I learned what it would take to forge ahead and dive deeper into the rich inner reserves and soul fertility of my Feminine Life Artistry. It is these women and their experiences I relied upon to light my way.

It is the collective synergy that created *Faces of the Mother* and is likewise what brought this book into being. By restoring faith in this and relying upon it, I opened to and repaired my connection with the wisdom asking to be expressed. In my willingness to be remade from the fabric of my most fearful place, I looked face-to-face at all areas where certain aspects of life were not an integral part of my nature. I learned to soften into the collective support that carried me on.

To partner with instead of resist my inner saboteur, and allow its stamina to naturally grow, is what brought this book into completion. I accepted that I felt stronger and more capable doing for others than doing for myself. Ahhh, the feminine way. Through non-resistance to my inherent nature, I learned to remember we are working together no matter how the outside form appears, and no matter what its face reflects. When I come from deep inside my creative genius, I bless life.

Because of the Feminine Life Artists in this book, I've had the courage to go forth. As I gaze at their art pieces and self-expression, carrying the knowing of their journeys deep within me, I feel something vast and untouched within. This helps me embrace and no longer resist self-limitation in following my creative purpose.

Our feminine restoration invites us to "embrace" and no longer "resist." And it is through and for this principle that this book is dedicated. In our culture we speak of 'beating resistance down' or 'breaking through our fear.' We claim 'when fear is present, love is absent.' To live in such a world, we've placed our hearts behind armor, creating a battle where none ever wants to exist. To live in such a world we've put our personal will forever at the forefront, constantly pushing against the current instead of flowing with the inherent way.

It does take great will and stamina to honestly look at patterns of our resistance to discover the unique way we each DO flow. Writing this book and supporting others upon this journey aided the dismantling of this tender terrain and allowed me to witness the process of the collective genius living inside our bodies, wombs and hearts. Moving through this experience with these Feminine Life Artists supported my original sense that it is our inner balancing and unification that allows us to grow into the people we most long to be.

Since childhood, I've carried the prayer to serve thy will. This is the ultimate way of the Mother. It has no logic and is barely conceivable in our current world conditions. It is for this that this book is written. The Mother is here, helping us bow our heads to peer into our hearts so we may know the terrain of love every step of the way.

May this journey provide something for and within you I could never have imagined. May it greet and embrace the deepest longing you've carried your whole life. May it aid you in your richest Soul Fertility.

With undying commitment to the well-being of us all.

What Is Your Deepest Longing For Yourself Now?

And so we end where we began, in the fire of our deepest longing... in the hunger of our soul's expression.

We breathe into this heart-aching place of feeling with all that we are and not running away. We let this moment and all it contains simply be so.

Here we are carried to the threshold of our greatest genius... into those places that until we're willing to tenderly hold in our hands and gaze at face-to-face, we will not serve the world in the courageous and most natural way we are each meant to. Here we face that the Mother and we are one.

In the Heart-Womb of Her almighty love, let yourself long and desire, wildly and deeply. Allow this soul fertility to heat and rise up from within. Feel it ignite inside your womb and by your free will. Tenderly cradle it in your own hands. Carry it all the way into the sacred chambers of yourself. Express what it does inside you, where it goes and how it travels. Carve, draw and sing out. Offer formation to this passionate love going on right now within your being. Your beloved co-creator is the source of creation itself coming alive through your body and breath, by your hands, heart and humor, from deep inside your belly and womb, in the fluidity of your blood and the fragility of your lovely bones.

Bring life alive! We all long to see this form of sacred expression being born through you.

Our Everlasting Hunger

And I asked because I longed to know... "What is your deepest longing for yourself now?"

And She answered through every one of us using Her one pure voice...

…the courage to keep digging, keep breathing, and the ability to accept the rewards of finding, and getting to keep, all the gold.

…a peaceful stretch. A project to look forward to.

…to remember this journey and the gentle reminder to trust myself. That there is so much beauty in not knowing where the path will lead me – my only job is to follow the "path" or even journey off of it when the inner knowing calls to me to do so... TRUST, it brings such a peace and a relief to think that I don't HAVE to know and it brings me into such a connected place with myself.

…that I can feel complete with this process. My product is my life, it is like the white canvas hanging on the wall in the modern art section – I hate that shit. I am really grappling with that: it feels like a copout. And yet, what I've experienced is real and there has been no space or the luxury of art. My life really is my art.

…honoring myself. Trusting myself. Remembering the strong woman I am.

…to enjoy my life to the fullest every moment of every day…slow down and be present. Our lives are so precious and sacred….

…I want my life to change—I want to live with true integrity and be able to provide for my family doing the things which make me happy. I want the world to change so that we all can do this.

…to continue to uncover and express creatively from deep within my soul. I am yearning to offer / be part of a group/ to explore / 'embodied awareness', presencing – sensing, creating, reflecting…'to play – express creatively with art supplies, music, dance'…to open more and more to love, intimacy…the beauty of life and relationships.

…to believe in myself. To have faith in who I am and what I do, and to know that my spirit is, in fact, part of something much greater or That Which Be.

…to continue to dive deep, to listen, to trust, to have courage and take risks. I want to believe and give what it is I am able to give as myself.

…to continue to grow and attempt to understand my journey and purpose here, on this tiny, blue globe, spinning in space.

…soulful expression, silence and noise. To use the time and gifts I have been given in passionate and meaningful ways. I really want to make it count!! To truly value my own unique expression enough to do it with any kind of regularity and a real and growing passion.

…to live as a sacred life artist…

~ OUR FEMININE LIFE ARTISTS

◌

Her Descent... a homecoming

I've come for silent retreat to a Trappist Abbey dedicated to the Mother. I've brought the knitted blue shawl from my mother's prayer group, and wrap it around me now. To this land I've ventured over the years to support my healing, reflection and contemplation. The most recent visit was upon completion of our *Faces of the Mother* journey. I wanted to commemorate our process and offer the sacred artistry of these women into the valley of my devotion.

Beyond the abbey there are acres upon acres of woods and trails. This land is known for its fertile soil and rich grape laden vineyards. Each time I've visited, my longing to find the monks' outdoor shrine to Our Lady of Guadalupe, the abbey's namesake, drew me into these forests. I'd walk for hours, following my intuition, traipsing over hillsides, upon trails and into dense forest, feeling my way towards this long sought-for destination. I'd never see another soul along my path. Eventually I'd turn back, not having found the shrine. My tiredness or an inner sense of completion would call me in. I'm sensitive about getting caught in 'endlessly searching' for fulfillment, and have always wanted to enjoy the path and discoveries right below my feet.

Yet, upon my return to the abbey, I'd notice a sense of failure arise, as if there was something I hadn't accomplished. The presence of the Mother would flow around and through me no matter where I ended. I was fed by and grateful for this.

That day last October when I came for closure and commemoration of our *Faces of the Mother* journey, something had shifted. It was my parents' anniversary. I was celebrating this sacred project I'd initiated and we'd now completed, and also the tender healing that comes with acceptance of one's life as it is. I felt the orchestration of creation's blessings. As I entered my room, I noticed a map on the desk. It was of the trails throughout the abbey's property, with a written description of how to get to the outdoor shrine. Though I know I'd looked at the map before, I hadn't paid it attention or chosen to take it as I walked. This time I put it in my pocket!

Walking in the crisp autumn air, I referred to the map to guide my way. I smiled. I was relying on and trusting a different aspect of wisdom. I no longer needed to judge where I longed to be or what would take me there. I would use whatever presented to support me. After more than an hour walking under the glaring sun up winding and secretive trails of a tree-laden hillside, I came to the outdoor shrine. Without fanfare, a circle of stones had been laid, and a structure of rocks placed one on top of another. An image of the Divine Mother rested at the top point with simple gifts and adornments tucked amongst the stones from those who had come before. If you weren't looking for the shrine, you'd walk right past it. A few bullet holes had been shot into the sign that led to this spot.

On this day of my parents' anniversary, I sit down on a rock in the sun and eat an orange. I found my way here in the only way that I could. Gentle tears fall. It didn't matter where I was. She is within me. Feminine grace carries me no matter where I end up. I feel the warmth of autumn upon my skin. Something has transformed. I turn my face towards the unfiltered scope of the sun and accept its warming rays.

I return again. It's summer the following year. As I arrive and walk up to the front desk, I let them know I'm here on personal retreat. "I'll be staying in Queen Anne's room." I stop and laugh. "Oh, I mean St. Anne's." The woman behind the desk laughs too. "Yes, the Queen's room!"

I walk through the entrance area that leads to the dining room, noticing a bulletin board filled with postcards, pictures and the quote-a-day calendar page for today. It reads, "In all faces is shown the Face of Faces, veiled and as if in a riddle." ~ St. Nicholas. We are brimming with and surrounded by the creativity of the universe, weaving it all together. I say a prayer to remain open to inspiration as I complete the *Faces of the Mother* manuscript.

I make my way up to St. Anne's room and feel a sense of familiarity. I give thanks to my maternal grandmother, Anna, for whom my mother and I share our middle name. I open the door placing my hand on the name placard. Anne was the mother of Mary, the blessed Mother and holy queen.

I remember as a girl crossing the wide bridge over a rapid flowing stream behind my grandmother's apartment. I'd stand there throwing leaves over one side, racing to the other to watch them move upon waters below. I'd make my way across the bridge to my grandmother's hillside grotto. It sat encircled by water, trees and stones. Here my grandmother tended her beloved roses. My mother   speaks of Babci's roses. She crushed eggshells and placed them around the base for nourishment. My mother named me after one of her mother's roses. I now live on the other side of the country from where my grandmother grew old. This is on opposite shores from where I was born. I now live in the City of Roses.

In my grandmother's garden was a statue of the Blessed Mother. I'd come here to pray and learn about my intimacy with the feminine. I was a girl who remembered the Mother's love and had innocent faith She would help me find my way. I was a daughter who felt an unquestionable intimacy with my inner wisdom, voice, blessings and care.

© CONNIE PETERS GULICK

I gather my things as I finish the last words of this book, ready to leave St. Anne's room. I will listen to the monks chant their devotion and prayers to the Mother. I will kneel and pray in my own way, knowing every one of us is precious. I will remember the prayers a circle of women have knitted into the shawl draped around my shoulders.

Sacred Chambers of my Creativity,
I plummet to the threshold that has no floor or foundation, to travel beyond
and into the joy and limitations of my body. Reveal to me where life begins.
Show me how love sustains itself. Make true and clear the framework of love's
vitality awakened through my form.

Holy Creator, I call out to you as a child who cannot find her way. I have
played along and at this journey of life, trying out things and possibilities,
putting on masks, hats and adornments. I have felt extreme emotions and
known no limit to where my mind and heart can travel. Take me now into
myself and myself alone. Help me feel the way creation courses through
my body and beyond, in ways that are natural, organic and sustainable
by my soul's recognition. Help me stand for and soften into this. Aid me in
surrendering to the power that creates my world in each moment.

I offer this body and the house of my origination to you. I reach out to share this with the earth, my source and all of creation. I give you my sacred uterus in service and devotion for life's holiest creating. Take precious care of it so I can learn to preserve it inside my own self. Reveal the tenderest places where I have denied my creativity's value, heritage and greatness. Place my uterus upon the altar of the Earth's heart so I might understand how to carry this reserve in the deepest heart of my own nature.

I pray with all that I am, from the place where I am that I am. Remake the structure of my body from the temple of love's sacred consecration. Aid me in welcoming this through every pore and cell of my flesh. Help me accept who I am to life. Be with me as I let the immaturity of any sense of my own worth descend into form.

Through the voice and medicine of my uterus, bring me home.

ᘓ

Can you hear Her calling? Can you hear Her calling, calling you home?

In this temple of creation's homecoming we find the many faces of the mother. We come to earth to love as only we can.

Rebirthing Ourselves, Rebirthing our World

I feel laughter arising. It's the kind that comes from deep inside. The type that's willing to take oneself lightly, and through such moments discovers you no longer feel tethered to anything of this world. This is the laughter that comes rolling in from the ocean, rising up in the belly like a soft, rhythmic and steady wave.

I remember this same feeling in labor. It arose with my initial contractions, beginning ever so subtly, yet with feelings like I'd be knocked over if I didn't stay completely connected and aware of myself and this process. I could feel every inch of those contractions and followed them from their beginnings, along my breath, up my spine, into the intense tightening of my abdomen that left me clutching for air and life. I recall hearing a voice tell me these contractions started in the origin of all things, and if I followed them into myself I would understand how life is constantly rebirthing us in each moment.

Can you hear Her calling? Can you hear Her calling, calling you home?

Our journey began in the sincerity and seriousness of our deepest longing and heart's vulnerability. And as all journeys do, it ends in the exact same place. We've come back to the point from which we started, making a full circle, returning to where we once stood looking upon a horizon, staring from atop a tree. As we peer out now, does anything feel or look different? Can we see more clearly? Do we believe we're purposelessly spinning on a frenzied wheel and can't find our way off? Do we feel we even need to get off the wheel anymore?

May this journey offer you renewed perspective... the kind that comes rolling in on the tides of the ocean, beginning in the true origination of life, carrying its breath, wisdom and activation all the way into and through your being and form. Can you receive this? Will you fully take it in?

May the cycles, rotations, circles and wheels of your life gently round out the hardest edges of self-judgment and doubt, so you may write simply because you can. So you may dance simply because you feel rhythm. So you may sing simply because you hear a tune. And may you rest in silence because there is nothing you must do to be you. May you create and birth as only you can, because you were designed for it. And may you love through it all because you were born to life.

Writing this book has taken me places I wasn't expecting to go, and as I welcome this, a full-bellied chuckle begins to flow through my body. I laugh, knowing this is exactly where I most longed to be!

In creating *Faces of the Mother*, I turned towards the face of love within myself, allowing the most painful, resistant, musty and terrorized aspects within me to simply be seen, held and embraced. There are things we are not meant to overcome. There are places in us we are not meant to transform. There are aspects of our world we are not meant to heal or perceive as needing to be changed.

Dearest Reader, this is where my love letter to you ends.

In transforming our relationship with the creative source within us, we discover we are the living vitality, breath and vessel of creation. And by peering into the heartache and wounds of our past and precognition, we accept we were designed to create as only we can, through the ways, rhythm and medium that is authentic and accurate for us, without judgment. Following our intimacy with the Mother allows us to remake our own relationship with how we give and receive love, and with how we value our intrinsic capacity to incubate, gestate and grow life. Through this inner quality of mothering, we learn an ancient power that we are *ALL* designed to use wisely and innocently, to bring life into its fullest manifestation in service and joy for it all.

As we access the heart of the Mother within, we live for the greater good without concern, and with mature awareness, of the ways we are each tending the well-being of ourselves and all others.

May your journey bring you home, into the love that is forever changing into the love that is changeless.

You will come to know Her completely as only you can know and love yourself. Savor this.

The Woman of the Eastern Peaks

Long ago and far away, in a land before this time, lived an ancient woman with cascading hair made of silver light and crystal gold. The woman's skin was clear and clean, reflecting luminosity of the fullest moon. Although her years were beyond what can be counted upon this earth, the woman's body was gentle and soft. Her movements fluid like a seahorse dancing in the sway of ocean's depth.

This ancient woman lived in a cottage perched high between eastern peaks, surrounded by quaking trees with roots descending to unshakable ground. The cottage was sparse... a wooden table and chair sat in the west, a soft downy mattress piled with quilted covers on the floor in the north, a sink and window facing the sun of the east, and the door of the cottage opened to greet the south. Upon entering this space, though no human before had, you were greeted by a brilliance even with so little inside. Light emanated from the hearth. A fire stone was at the center... always glowing and warm, tended by this woman's hands streaked with veins of rambling rivers moving across plains.

This ancient woman's days consisted of waking to morning light, rising to tend flames of the fire, preparing foods gathered from plants and spaces encircling the cottage, and being with the neighboring animals.

The silver-gold haired woman spent her time quietly in the forest with deer, scurrying over ground with the squirrels, and scratching her back, resting against trees' bark with bear. She spent her days listening... and waiting. Waiting for a time when, like her cottage door opening to the south, she would be called to venture from this circle into all that lay beyond.

How she knew when the time would come arose in her listening. The ancient woman walked barefoot so she could feel what dirt wanted her to know. She threw her hands into the wind to sense the singing of air. She placed her ear against oak and maple to listen to the process of shedding bark. This supported her through her days in becoming.

As the woman moved about now, the air felt crisp, biting her skin. The ground below was brittle and crackled as she walked. Tree limbs swayed freely in a quickening wind, unattached to anything but their solid trunk. The woman felt the essence of Winter rise and fall as she listened to these sights and sounds, old and familiar. And this time her listening brought forth something else... something new. The land was beginning to vibrate with the sound of a season she had never heard before.

For several days the woman continued to watch and listen. Signs of when, where and how were rooted deep, coursing through rich blood into her hands and feet. She knew the time would come when she would quietly close up the cottage, taking fire with her to travel these eastern peaks back into valleys below and beyond. Her belly, warmed by such embers, knew.

After weeks of noticing this newness, the woman looked into the horizon to gaze at the oak meadow now sparkling with fresh snow. She watched a shift beginning high in the sky. Snow that had fallen fast and heavy at daybreak was now slowing. Crystal flakes descending to earth's floor began to rise and float. White shining particles held still in the space around her... twirling, spinning, becoming wings that glistened.

The ancient woman reached out her hand. The snowflakes would not land! They moved, caressing her fingertips, beckoning rhythm and dance. The woman started to laugh. Sound cascaded deep from her belly, and a color not there before entered her eyes.

"Is it time?" she asked, like a child who already knows but goes through the questioning anyway.

Snowflakes swirled with intensity, up and down her arms, around her head, lightly kissing the lids of her eyes. The woman let out a breath... long, slow and deep. A few flakes moved closer to catch the release of her air, riding it into the distance.

The woman turned and began to walk back to the cottage. It was time.

Standing in the heart of the room, at center, she picked up a cream-colored cloth she'd been sewing, a few stitches each day over all these years. This fabric, persistently tended, had now become a bag.

The woman sat down at the table in the chair, and picked up her needle. A spindly, sturdy golden thread she wove through the seam at the top, and stretched it's opening wide in preparation. She moved to the fire, reaching towards kindled coals at the bottom. Her weathered hands searching for sparks that remained lit, to the embers she had used each day to light her fire and keep it sustained.

The woman placed these embers in the bag and pulled the golden cord tight. She walked out of the cabin, closing the door behind her. Surrounded by winter's clear air, watching snow crystals move in circular patterns, she questioned, "How will I share these embers?"

The ancient woman of the eastern peaks had spent her days, an eternity, attuning her rhythm to hear the message... to know the time. She had trusted this listening.

Snowflakes twirled in new patterns, different each moment from the ones before. The woman noticed. In her chest a burning sensation rose, spreading throughout her form. At first filled with a reddish fire, it then softened to iridescent wings alighting on air.

The woman sensed gentle sounds, voices moving towards her in the wind. She turned an attuned ear to the south and listened, "Inside your heart these embers live. You will listen to the earth within you now, and be guided as you always have by the universal rhythm. The illumination of your tended fire will be received. It will be seen by those who use vision to see. It will be heard in sound by those who use hearing to hear. It will be felt in a warm caress by those who use feeling to feel. It will become a settling breath to those who find presence in being. Walk forward, onward, into the direction of the softening wind."

The ancient woman began walking, leaving footprints behind her. She headed south from this land of the east, a golden-threaded bag over her shoulder, a luminous face peering into valleys beyond.

❧

Our Feminine Life Artists

Mother as Mystic

LORI WOOLF has been making art and mixing potions since she was a kid. She continues her happy alchemy practice in Portland, Oregon.

Mother as Artist & Creatress

JEWELZ ANN LOVEJOY was awarded to the Portland Art Institute on scholarship, and later passed on her acceptance, believing being an artist was not a valued profession. She learned to channel her creativity through hair artistry, designing and visioning styles to help people express and bridge their inner and outer self-image. She chose additional studies that modeled pathways of deep growth: Kundalini meditation, Reiki, American-Celtic Shamanism, Esthetic certification and licensing, and earth-based Goddess empowerment, creating ceremonies and a sisterhood of never ending circles. Jewelz became a Djembe drumming leader and woman's Motocross racer for off-road dirt biking. She now calls all this life experience "Priestess her'art healing" and her mission is, "Opening to Authentic Beauty and profound Self-love".

Mother as Healer

KRISIEY SALSA is nourished by learning and loving. Her approach to change is mindful, compassionate, positive and patient. She is not afraid to dig deep inside herself or connect deeply to others. Krisiey finds herself nourished by the connections she makes with others, the lessons she learns through self-exploration and the change she can offer to the world through mindful living. She endeavors to be creative, daring, forthright, funny, feisty, graceful, passionate and authentic. Her energy is derived from exploring her passions, like food, health, dancing and photography, and from challenging herself to expand her boundaries. Krisiey feels compelled to do more – to do good things for the world – to make this one beautiful life she has count. Learn more about her and her photography at www.aomephoto.com.

Mother as Distiller

SARAH PAGE lives in Portland, Oregon with her husband, two children and two cats. She believes life can be distilled into one simple truth: Love is stronger than anything. She also thinks it's really important to acknowledge people and thanks her Sister Mothers in this project and beyond for their guidance.

Mother as Decomposer

HOLLY HINSON discovered her inner artist when she was pregnant with her twin girls. Bed-bound for four months, she started making origami balls and found a healing in her creations. She has since embraced herself as an artist and enjoys all forms of creating. Holly is thrilled to be able to combine her passions in her work as a chocolate maker. She also enjoys learning from her children and witnessing their boundless creativity and lust for life.

Mother as Midwife

ANNA KRISTINA SODERBERG is a magical mother of two incredible spirits and lives within the swirling universe in a place called Portland. She is a student midwife at Birthingway College of Midwifery and also is a lactation specialist. She writes poetry, sings songs and nurtures edible plants in her garden, where weeds wind all around.

Mother as Leader

CATHERINE GEE gravitates to both right and left-brain ways of being and doing. She is a teacher and student of life. As a leader, facilitator and coach, she quietly listens, provides a calm and creative space for reflection, inspiring connection to Source and one's Life Force. In creating a learning environment, she shares transformative practices for others to develop their own leadership presence. In this space, be inspired to connect with your own inner essence, wisdom, and vision. From this place, take action, raise your vibration and your voice! Visit Catherine at www.AlchemyofU.com.

Mother as Regenerator

CATHERINE DART has always been drawn to the arts—from her explorations as a child to her degree in Theatre to discovering oil painting in Santa Fe and stone carving in New York City. Throughout, she has found that all these mediums have deepened her understanding of herself and the surrounding world, helping her to draw from her inner questions and answers and manifest them in form. She is happily married to her high school sweetheart and is the mother of two children—two great works in and of themselves.

Mother as Priestess

DANA GILLEM KLAEBE has a degree in painting from the University of North Carolina at Pembroke. For 30 years she has concentrated her creative efforts on painting and mixed media. Her work is primarily influenced by mythology, decorative arts and expressionists, as well as crows, ravens and magpies – all collectors of shiny, sparkly things. Her paintings are the result of a lengthy process of building surfaces, reducing those surfaces and recreating them over and over, until surface and meaning are revealed. Armed with a power sander and boxes of golden glitter and paint, each work reveals shimmering secrets of distant places and time.

Mother as Bestower & Beloved

CONNIE PETERS GULICK began her journey towards beauty at a young age when she first noticed a leaf imprint on the sidewalk. Her interest in designing and making things has led to adventures such as starting an art program at an inner city school, opening a flower shop, managing an Asian furniture showroom, and showing art pieces locally. Currently working in the field of natural health, she is also a student of Reiki. Participating in this project is an incredible opportunity to deepen her artistic expression and to expand as a person. Connie is a lover of Divine and the ways this relationship plays out with others as well as ourselves. She continues to find both marriage and the process of creating to be powerful initiations. In 2013, Connie took an additional name of Aquila. She and her husband, Rall Rexoris, wish to bless the world through their union. Visit Connie at www.aquilaenchantra.com.

Mother as Unifier

You, me, she, he, us, we... all of us, everyone, everything, everywhere.

Send us images and expressions of your Unified Self to:
sharonannrose3@gmail.com

Thank you for joining us upon this journey!

❧
Thank You xo

Have you ever had that feeling of crumpling to the ground? As if you no longer can hold yourself up, while some inner dam opens and a cascade of water pours over without distinction. It's not exhaustion, helplessness, or even apathy this brings forth. It's a feeling of dissolution and surrender... falling into what's been supporting you all along. Out of this I share thanks for all that's supported *Faces of the Mother*.

I begin in my heart, honoring this wild impulse that drives me to return to the origination of things, into the primordial place that existed before I knew I was. I honor all that's created me, even when I didn't want to be her.

I honor the Feminine Life Artists who heard my call within their hearts and stepped into this with determination, trepidation and sisterhood. Thank you to Lori, Jewelz, Krisiey, Sarah, Holly, Anna, Catherine G., Catherine D., Dana, Connie & Jacinda. You came forth with dignity and faith, and your trust propelled my commitment in to the woman I am becoming. The image of us standing in circle, candles of all colors glowing at center, singing from our hearts, lives deeply within me.

I honor the Sisterhood of our Feminine Temple in Portland at the Sweet Nest. Through this experiential web of Sacred Feminine crafting, I learned to trust the flow of love and life, and discovered the Temple that lives within. And to the Masonic Lodge and Brotherhood, for standing around us as we learned to rest and be poised at center, just as we are.

To Karen Latvala, my editor and long-time family friend. You reentered my world as I learned to trust these cycles of life that will forever move beyond my comprehension. You supported me to breathe in to the care of the wise women that surround me.

To my graphic designer, Lanz Travers, who has a depth of heart so rare in this world. I have no words for what your presence in my life and on this project has meant. You know how to cradle the heart of the world in your own.

I honor the many women, mothers, couples and kin who've opened their heroic stories to me, imbuing my sense of purpose and resiliency. There is no end to my gratitude for the depth of wisdom, heartache, tenderness, beauty and strength you've revealed. I want to acknowledge treasures amongst these ~ Annie Ray, Darleen Sumner, Ana Azizkhani, Jenny Rayfield, Jennifer Peck & Tanyia Jean Hall, true leaders in the ways of the Feminine heart.

I place my forehead upon the earth for this life and those who've chosen to be with me in its crafting. To my ancestors and future lineage, to my mother and father – Jane & Bill, my sisters – Debi, Sue & Karen Sophia, my niece Danielle Mercedes, and my brother-in-law, Dan. And for my ancestors, especially my grandmothers, Felixia and Anna, thank you for guiding me from the land of spirit. I draw upon your voices every step of the way.

To my mother-in-law, Mildred, thank you for role modeling your grace and strength. And to the Wease family for welcoming me with open arms.

To special and inspiring women in my life who've elevated mothering to a sacred art, upholding protection of the innocence that ignites the fire in my belly ~ Lisa Benitez, Meladee Martin, Lorie Clements, Carol Kerschner, Angela Kemling & Cheri Vawter.

To my Aries-Scorpio sister Jasmina Soleil, you are a light of the sun that reminds me to see the brightness in myself, holding steady through the storm.

To my beloved soul sister, Jewelz Ann Lovejoy, who sang through your tears when I forgot what I stood for. Your presence and friendship remind me to always live for love.

And to the Women of the Wild Heart... who gathered around me in the fire of their being, while I took the final steps to bring this book to the world. I drew upon your courage every step of the way. Thank you to my Sister Intimate, Jenny, for courageously singing our redemption song.

To those who call me Mother ~ Kalen, Kordan, Etian & my spirit children ~ you trusted the impulse of creation through me even as I resisted. Your beauty, development and path deepen me into what's most important.

And to Peter, the one I am known to as lover, wife, partner, instigator, foe and friend, what we've lived through will never be contained or explained by this world. I trust in our hearts and God's embrace to hold us through all to come.

To the Source of all things, the sacred Mother and Father, I tremble with thanksgiving for being alive and having this purpose.

Resources & Credits

ACKNOWLEDGING ALL WHO SUPPORTED THIS BOOK'S BIRTHING INTO FORM

GRAPHIC DESIGN: Lanz Travers, Masha Shubin

PHOTOGRAPHY: Krisiey Salsa, Apple of My Eye Photography ~ www.aomephoto.com
Connie Peters Gulick, Aquila Enchantra ~ www.aquilaenchantra.com
Kristal Passy, Kristal Passy Photography ~ www.kristalpassy.com

EDITOR-IN-CHIEF: Karen Latvala

REVIEWERS: Ariel Spilsbury, Anaiya Sophia, Devaa Hailey Mitchell, Karen Latvala, Joyce Vissell, Holly Zapf, Jasmin Soleil, Lynda Terry & Robin Bodhi

FOREWORD: Jasmin Soleil ~ www.jasminsoleil.com

PUBLISHER: Inkwater Press, Portland, OR ~ www.inkwater.com

ADDITIONAL RESOURCES:

Anaiya Sophia & Carriers of the Flame
www.anaiyasophia.com/

Ariel Spilsbury & the 13 Moon Mystery School
www.holographicgoddess.com
www.13moonmysteryschool.org

Omiza River
www.omizariver.com

About the Author

Sharon Ann Rose resides in Portland, Oregon on an urban farm with her husband, 3 boys and a circle of companion creatures. Here she stands rooted and unfettered, watching sunrises through the forest scape, and leaning in to the towering fir trees that surround her yard.

© KRISTAL PASSY

Sharon is a mother, author and Feminine Wisdom Guide. She supports women through inner initiation into their creative source connection through ceremonies, trainings, online programs and mentorship.

Faces of the Mother is her first book.

Sharon Ann Rose
sharonannrose3@gmail.com
www.sharonannrose.com

The Amansala Foundation

A percentage of all profits from the sale of this book will be invested in *The Amansala Foundation*, to support the creative expression and endeavors of Feminine Life Artists.

"*Amansala*" in sanskrit means '*a state of tranquility by the water*,' and is the initiation Sharon underwent through pregnancy, birth and raising her 3 sons. It was during her third son's birth that she learned to value, trust and honor her own creative process, its unique expression and way of manifestation. From this seed of literal and internal rebirth, the dream of *The Amansala Foundation* rooted, following a current of reverence for the feminine way of creating. Out of this, Sharon wishes to bless and stand beside others as they reclaim their inherent, innocent and unique way of the force and flow of life and love moving through them.

Each year *The Amansala Foundation* will donate a percentage of *Faces of the Mother* sales to individuals and organizations blessing the world with their inherent expression of creation. Your suggestion of such individuals and organizations are welcomed.

You may reach *The Amansala Foundation* at the contact info listed for Sharon.

CPSIA information can be obtained
at www.ICGtesting.com
Printed in the USA
FSOW04n1330230317
32046FS